TinkerActive
WORKBOOKS

KINDERGARTEN · MATH · AGES 5–6

by Nathalie Le Du

illustrated by Ellen Stubbings

educational consulting by Randi House

 Odd Dot · New York

Classifying & Sorting

Look at each street in Tinker Town. Circle the objects that are the same.

Count each group. Then trace each number and say it aloud.

Look at the parking lot. Circle the vehicle in each row that does not match.

Find 2 objects in your home that are the same, and draw them. Then draw 1 object that is different.

Same	Same	Not the Same

Draw a line to match the objects in the cart to the similar objects on the shelf.

After each match, fill in the missing words and say this sentence aloud: These are the same, but this one is _____, and this one is _____.

It's Career Day, and the MotMots have dressed up as their favorite community helpers. Draw a line to match the MotMot with his or her missing tool.

Count how much treasure each MotMot has. Then draw a line from each MotMot to the treasure chest with the matching number.

Look at the pair of objects and then circle the object that belongs in this group. Say aloud why these objects should be grouped together.

Look in a closet, cabinet, or dresser. How are the objects grouped together? Are all the socks together? Or are all the winter clothes together? Can you sort the objects in different ways?

LET'S START!

Construction paper
(at least 4 different colors)

Small items like:
buttons, rocks, blocks, coins, beans,
pasta shells, figurines, toy cars

Bag or pillowcase

Markers and/or crayons

Chalk

4 cardboard boxes or cereal boxes

LET'S TINKER!

Lay each sheet of construction paper out in front of you.

Put the small objects in a bag or pillowcase and shake them up. **Pull** 1 item out at a time and place it on the matching colored construction paper. If the object doesn't match any color, **make** a group next to the construction paper. **Continue** matching until your bag is empty.

Think of other ways you could sort these objects. **Label** the construction paper and make up your own sorting game! Or **gather** another pillowcase full of objects and race a friend—
who can sort objects the
fastest?

LET'S MAKE: SIDEWALK GAME!

1. **Draw** your own number chart using chalk.

2. **Collect** objects that are the same or similar.

3. **Put** the correct number of objects underneath each number in your chart.

LET'S ENGINEER!

The landfill in Tinker Town is filling up—fast! Dimitri wants to start a recycling program, but the MotMots aren't very good at sorting paper, glass, metal, and plastic.

How can Dimitri show other MotMots how to sort different objects?

Think of a way to show others how to sort paper, glass, metal, and plastic objects into different bins.

Use your cardboard boxes as your bins. How will someone know where to put a bottle, piece of paper, can, or other trash?

PROJECT 1: DONE!
Get your sticker!

Counting & Quantities

Count the number of objects aloud. Then trace the number.

1
cake

2
cards

3
pizzas

4
party horns

5
candles

hats

balloons

bubbles

sundaes

gifts

How many dots are on each painting? Draw a line to the correct number and then trace the number.

 The MotMots love to count aloud and clap. If the MotMots are counting the dots, how many times should they clap for each painting? Clap and count each group of dots aloud.

Follow each animal's tracks. How many footprints did each animal leave? Count the number of footprints and then write the number.

Try counting your own steps while you walk. How many steps does it take for you to go from one place to another?

LET'S START!

10 or more buttons, pebbles, dried pasta, or coins

Construction paper

Pencils or crayons

Scissors
(with an adult's help)

Glue

Chalk

LET'S TINKER!

Choose 1 type of object, such as pebbles, dried pasta, or buttons.

Count how many you have.

Arrange the group in different ways: scattered, in a circle, in a line, or in another way you create. What happens to the number of objects? Does it change or stay the same?

LET'S MAKE: FINGER COUNTER!

1. Trace 1 hand onto construction paper.

2. Cut it out.

3. **Glue** only the palm down on another piece of construction paper and let it dry.

4. **Show** the number 1 by bending the fingers. Then **show** the numbers 2, 3, 4, and 5. **Count** up and down using the finger-counting mat. Can you show zero?

5. If counting to 5 with one hand is easy, **trace** your other hand, cut it out, and glue down the palm. Then **show** the numbers zero to 10!

LET'S ENGINEER!

The MotMots love to race! But they aren't very good at directions.

How can the MotMots make a racecourse so they know where to step next?

Design a 10-step racecourse that a MotMot can follow step-by-step. **Use** objects to create a path. How many objects will you need? What happens to the number of steps if you change the direction of the racecourse?

PROJECT 2: DONE!
Get your sticker!

Circle a group of 10 pandas on each tree. Then count how many pandas are left over. Last, trace the total number of pandas on each tree.

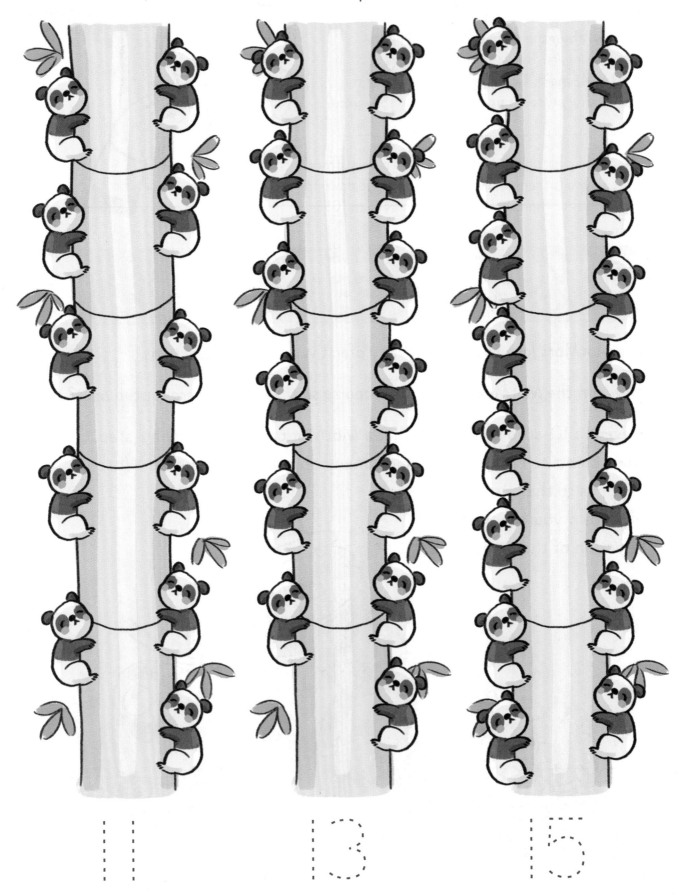

11   13   15

Fill in or trace the missing numbers. Then read numbers 1 through 20 aloud.

1 2 ___ ___ 5

6 ___ ___ ___ 9

11 12 13 14 15

16 17 18 19 20

Callie sells seashells by the seashore! Count the seashells aloud and fill in the missing number. Then count the other objects in each group aloud and write the number.

Callie sells _____ seashells by the seashore!

_____ starfish

_____ blue sunglasses

1, 2, 3, 4, 5, 6, 7, 8, 9, 10,
11, 12, 13, 14, 15, 16, 17, 18, 19, 20

_____ sailboats

_____ swimmers

_____ turtles

_____ sand castles

_____ sandals

SANDALS

Read the numbers 1 through 20 aloud and answer each question.

What number is Enid standing on?

_____

What number is this MotMot standing on?

_____

If a MotMot is standing on number **10**, what number comes next? _____

If a MotMot is standing on number **18**, what number comes next? _____

If a MotMot is standing on number **15**, what number comes next? _____

What number is Callie standing on?

_____

14

12

15

16

What number is Brian standing on?

_____

19

What number is this dog standing on?

_____

18

Make your own number path! Write numbers 1 through 20 on different sheets of paper, then arrange them in order throughout your home or outside. Do you know what number to step on next?

LET'S START!

GATHER THESE TOOLS AND MATERIALS.

20 small items like:
cotton balls, beans, buttons, paper clips, bobby pins, pebbles

Empty egg carton

Craft sticks

Tape

Empty plastic bottles

Construction paper

Old oatmeal containers, cereal boxes, or small cardboard boxes

Markers, crayons, or paint

LET'S TINKER!

Drop each small object one by one into a bucket, sink, bathtub, or other body of water. What do you see? What do you hear? Can you use the sights and sounds to help you count the objects?

LET'S MAKE: TINKER TOOLBOX!

1. **Decorate** an egg carton or make a container with separate sections.

2. Then **separate** your objects into groups— group all the paper clips together, group all the beans together, and so on.

3. **Count** how many objects are in each group, put them inside the separate sections, and write the number of objects on your container.

LET'S ENGINEER!

The MotMots are going on a trip across a big lake. They want to take 20 gifts to their 20 friends on the other side.

How can they cross the lake without getting their gifts wet?

Build something that would keep 20 objects dry as it floats across water.

Count your objects as you put them on or inside your vehicle. Then **float** your vehicle on water. Did you make it to 20 objects? Or did your vehicle sink? If so, at what number?

Keep trying until you make a vehicle that can hold 20 objects!

PROJECT 3: DONE!
Get your sticker!

Counting to 50 by Ones

Read the numbers 1 through 50 aloud, and trace the missing numbers. Then color-by-number to reveal a picture.

1	2	3	4	5
6	7	8	9	10
11	12	13	14	15
16	17	18	19	20
21	22	23	24	25
26	27	28	29	30
31	32	33	34	35
36	37	38	39	40
41	42	43	44	45
46	47	48	49	50

PINK:

1, 3, 5, 6, 7, 8, 9, 10, 11, 12, 13, 14, 15, 17, 18, 19

BLUE:

2, 4, 16, 20, 21, 22, 24, 25, 26, 27, 29, 30, 31, 32, 35, 36, 37, 39, 40, 41, 44, 45, 46, 47, 49, 50

GREEN:

23, 28, 33, 34, 38, 42, 43, 48

What number comes before, and what number comes after? Fill in the missing numbers in each row.

19   20   _____

29   _____   31

34   35   _____

44   _____   46

48   49   _____

Connect the dots by drawing a line from 1 through 25 in order.
Say each number aloud.

Connect the dots by drawing a line from 26 through 50 in order. Say each number aloud.

These MotMots are 50 years old! What do you want to do when you are 50 years old? Tell someone a story that begins, "When I am 50 years old, I want to . . ."

Read the numbers 21 through 50 aloud, and answer each question.

What number is Amelia standing on?

_____

What number is this rabbit standing on?

_____

What number is Dimitri standing on?

_____

If a MotMot is standing on number **29**, what number comes next? _____

If a MotMot is standing on number **40**, what number comes next? _____

If a MotMot is standing on number **49**, what number comes next? _____

50

48 49

What number is
Frank sitting on?

_____

46

45 44 43

42

41

40

What number is this
MotMot standing on?

_____

36 37 38

Carefully remove pages 22, 23, 30, and 31. Then lay
them side by side to see all 50 steps through Tinker Town!
Count all 50 steps aloud. Where can *you* walk in 50 steps?
Give it a try and find out!

LET'S START!

GATHER THESE TOOLS AND MATERIALS.

2 dice

Crayons and markers

50 small items like:
dried pasta, beads, bolts, washers, cereal, pretzels

Construction paper

String

Scissors
(with an adult's help)

Old plain light-colored T-shirt

Cardboard

LET'S TINKER!

Roll the dice and put the numbers side-by-side. For example, if you roll a 2 and a 4, your number is 24.

Show your number in 3 unique ways.

Do the same for the number before and the number after. If your number is 24, show numbers 23 and 25, too!

LET'S MAKE: NUMBER FASHION!

Choose your favorite number between 1 and 50. Then **choose** either a necklace or a T-shirt—or make both!

For the number necklace:

1. Cut a very long piece of string, about the length of your arm.

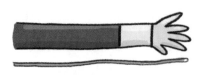

2. Tie a knot at one end.

3. String up to 50 pieces of dried pasta, beads, or whatever your small objects are on it. Love the number 22? **String** 22 beads while counting aloud.

4. Tie the 2 sides together for a necklace.

For the number T-shirt:

1. Put the cardboard inside the T-shirt so the marker doesn't bleed through.

2. Grab a marker. Either **write** the numbers 1 through 50 on the T-shirt, or draw up to 50 of your favorite things while counting aloud. Love the number 33? Love ice cream? **Draw** 33 ice-cream cones or 1 giant ice-cream cone with 33 sprinkles on it.

LET'S ENGINEER!

The MotMots were on their way to the craft market in Craft County to sell their number necklaces. They were almost there when they realized they forgot their pencils and paper! Oh no!

How can they keep track of how many necklaces they sell?

Make something that can be used to keep count up to 50. **Use** your small items to represent the necklaces that were sold.

PROJECT 4: DONE!
Get your sticker!

Counting to 100 by Tens

Trace the missing numbers. Then answer the questions.

1	2	3	4	5	6	7	8	9	
11	12	13	14	15	16	17	18	19	20
	22	23	24	25	26	27	28	29	30
31	32	33	34	35	36	37	38	39	40
41	42	43	44	45	46	47	48	49	50
51	52	53	54	55	56	57	58	59	60
	62	63	64	65	66	67	68	69	70
71	72	73	74	75	76	77	78	79	80
81	82	83	84	85	86	87	88	89	90
91	92	93	94	95	96	97	98	99	100

What number is the watermelon on? _____

What number comes next? _____

What number is the picnic basket on? _____

What number comes before? _____

What number is the food plate on? _____

What number comes before? _____

The objects are in groups of 10. Count the objects by tens and then write the number.

Help the MotMots reach the other side of Mount Ten!
Count by tens up to 100 aloud and write the missing numbers.
Then count by tens down to zero aloud and write the missing numbers.

While hiking, the MotMots gather supplies for their campsite.
How many groups of 10 objects do they have?

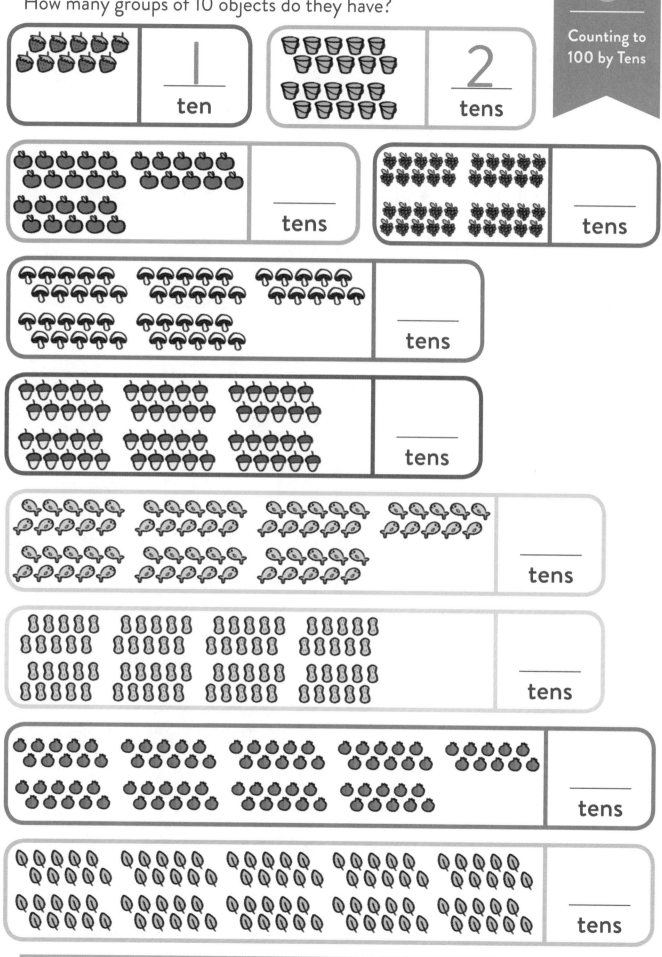

_1_ ten

_2_ tens

___ tens

___ tens

___ tens

___ tens

___ tens

___ tens

___ tens

___ tens

Why is it helpful to count items by tens? What kinds of things do you count by tens?

Count by tens, and fill in the blanks.

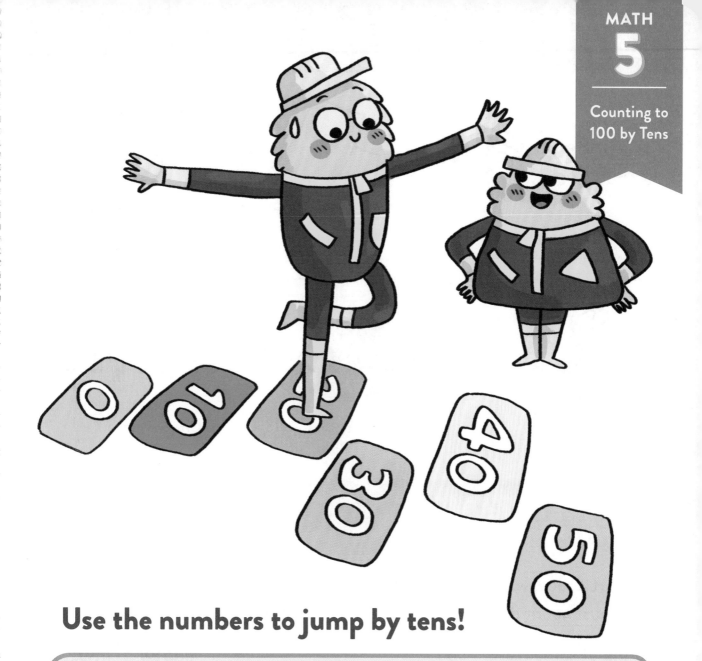

Use the numbers to jump by tens!

1. First, find a partner to play with.

2. Then, cut out the numbers on page 38 with an adult's help and place them on the floor in order.

3. One player shouts the starting number and whether the other player will jump up or down by tens. For example, one player shouts, "Twenty up!" and the other player jumps on 20, 30, 40, and 50! Or a player can shout, "Forty down!" and the other player jumps on 40, 30, 20, 10, and zero.

4. Take turns choosing the starting number and direction.

5. If you want to make it more difficult, make your own jumping squares for 60, 70, 80, 90, and 100.

Up to 55 small items like:
blocks, beans, raisins, macaroni, beads

White paper

Construction paper

Scissors
(with an adult's help)

Old toys and clothes

Crayons or markers

LET'S TINKER!

To start a race, you must count down: 3, 2, 1, go! To launch a rocket, you also must count down: 10, 9, 8, 7, 6, 5, 4, 3, 2, 1, liftoff!

Think of some reasons you might count down from 100 by tens.

Imagine a reason and use your objects to show counting down by tens.

100...90...
80...70...
60...50...
40...30...

LET'S MAKE: YOUR OWN MONEY!

Use tens to make your own money: $10, $20, $30, and so on, up to $100.

Design and draw your money. What will your money look like? What can you do to make your money easy to count? How could you design your money so everyone knows how much it's worth? Why might you use tens for money—why not a smaller number or a larger number?

LET'S ENGINEER!

The MotMots love garage sales! They have lots to sell but they only have price tags that say zero.

How can they change the price tags so they can charge some money?

Gather some things to sell. **Fill** in how much each item costs on the price tag stickers from page 385. What happens if you write a number before the zero? Then **sticker** your items. **Find** a friend or an adult and pretend to sell and buy the items. You can use the money you made in the last exercise to buy and sell!

PROJECT 5: DONE!
Get your sticker!

Comparing Quantities & Numbers

Draw lines to match each 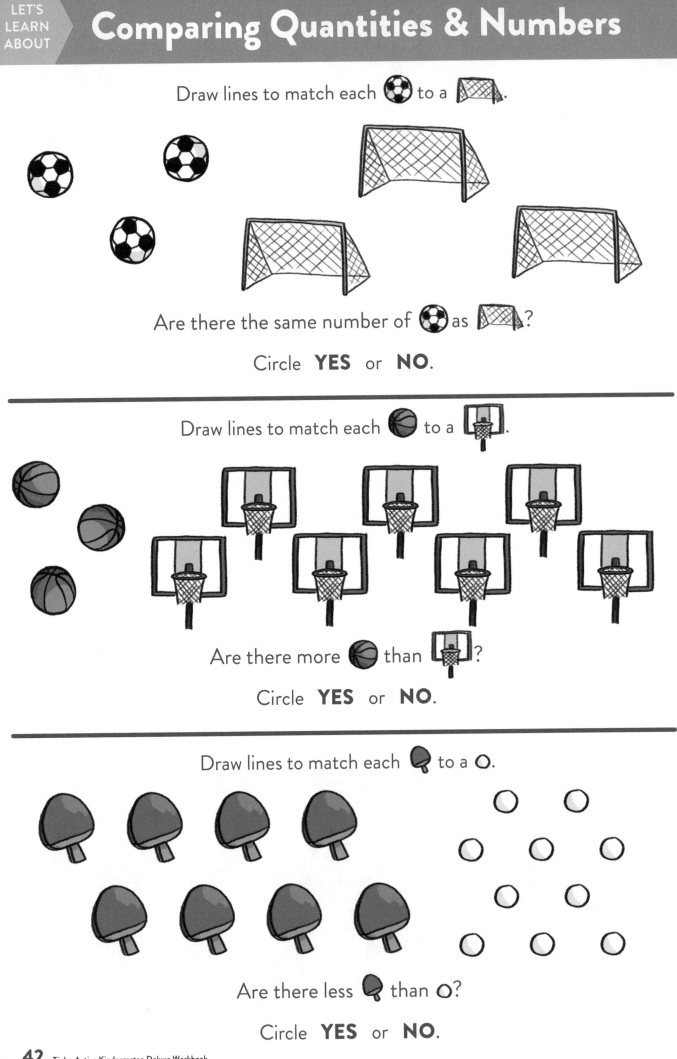 to a .

Are there the same number of as ?

Circle **YES** or **NO**.

Draw lines to match each to a .

Are there more than ?

Circle **YES** or **NO**.

Draw lines to match each to a O.

Are there less than O?

Circle **YES** or **NO**.

Draw lines to match each 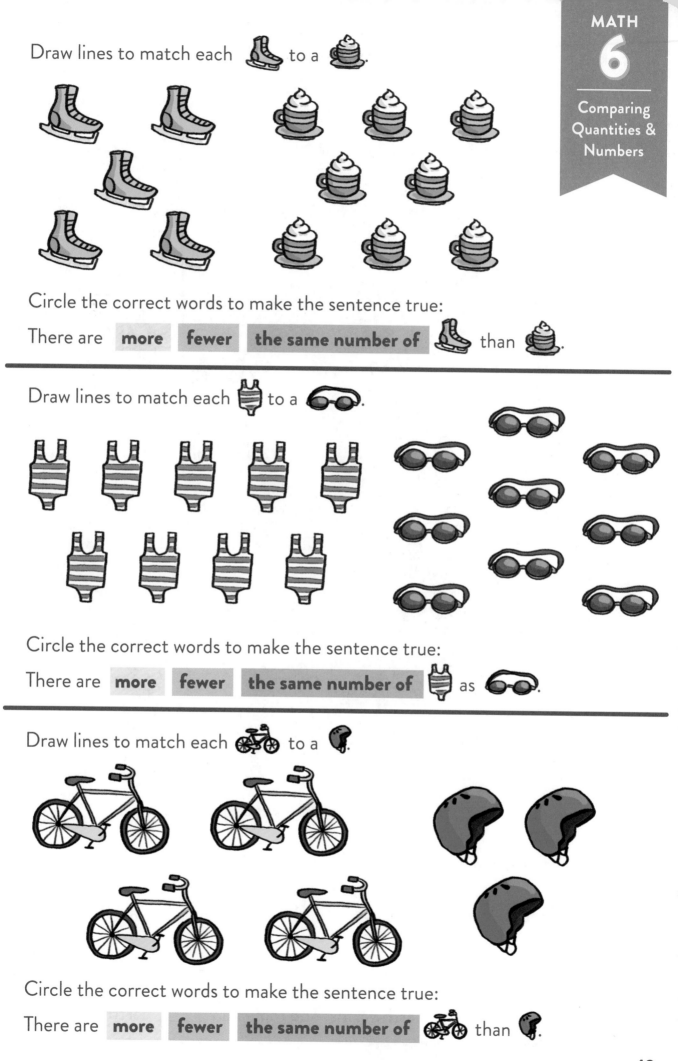 to a .

Circle the correct words to make the sentence true:

There are   **more**   **fewer**   **the same number of**   than .

Draw lines to match each to a .

Circle the correct words to make the sentence true:

There are   **more**   **fewer**   **the same number of**   as .

Draw lines to match each to a .

Circle the correct words to make the sentence true:

There are   **more**   **fewer**   **the same number of**   than .

Look at the picture. Then read the beginning of the story aloud and write the missing number to make each sentence true.

One fall day, the forest animals were getting ready for winter.

The squirrel found _____ acorns. The woodpecker stored _____ acorns.

The mouse carried _____ berries. The deer had _____ berries.

The ant dragged _____ leaf. The sheep had _____ leaves.

The blue bird caught _____ earthworms. The mole had _____ earthworms, too.

Finish the story. Circle **more**, **fewer**, or **the same number of** to make each sentence true.

When winter came along, the weather turned cold. There was snow on the ground and no food to be found. Everyone was hungry!

The squirrel had **more** **fewer** **the same number of** acorns than the woodpecker. So the squirrel shared with the woodpecker.

The mouse had **more** **fewer** **the same number of** berries than the deer. So the deer shared with the mouse.

The ant had **more** **fewer** **the same number of** leaves than the sheep. So the sheep shared with the ant.

The blue bird had **more** **fewer** **the same number of** earthworms as the mole. So they happily ate together!

Draw a line through the maze so that each MotMot buys the correct number of vegetables. Brian wants to buy **fewer than 2** . Callie wants to buy **more than 3** .

Count each set of objects and write the number.

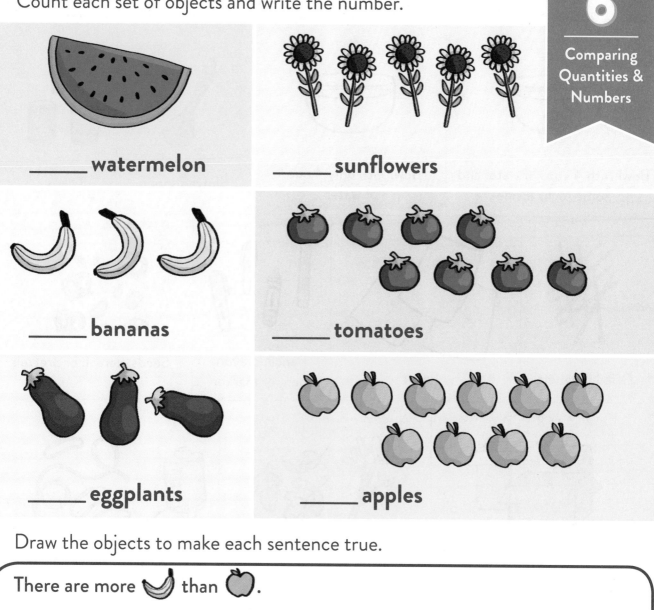

_____ watermelon

_____ sunflowers

_____ bananas

_____ tomatoes

_____ eggplants

_____ apples

Draw the objects to make each sentence true.

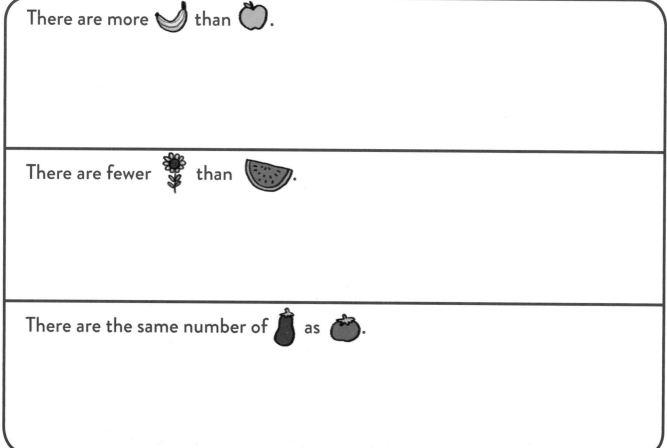

There are more 🍌 than 🍎.

There are fewer 🌻 than 🍉.

There are the same number of 🍆 as 🍅.

LET'S START!

GATHER THESE TOOLS AND MATERIALS.

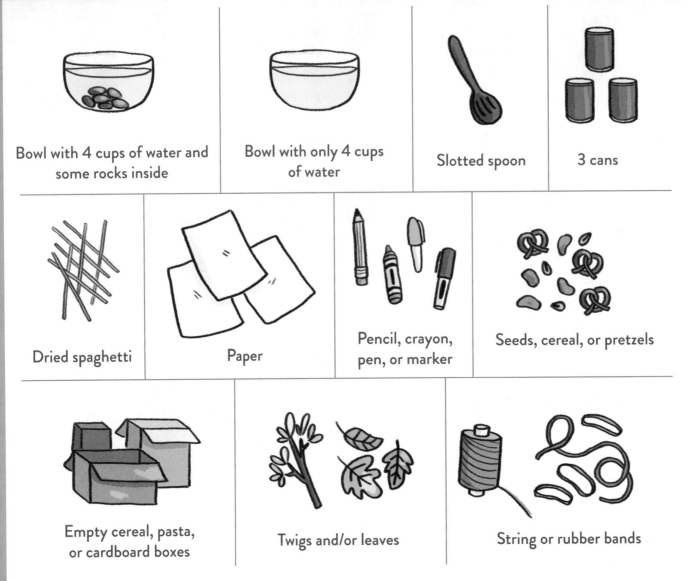

Bowl with 4 cups of water and some rocks inside

Bowl with only 4 cups of water

Slotted spoon

3 cans

Dried spaghetti

Paper

Pencil, crayon, pen, or marker

Seeds, cereal, or pretzels

Empty cereal, pasta, or cardboard boxes

Twigs and/or leaves

String or rubber bands

LET'S TINKER!

Put your bowl of rocks and bowl of water next to each other. Using the slotted spoon, **carry** some of the rocks over to the other bowl. Which has more rocks now? Does one bowl have more water than the other? If anything changed, why do you think that is?

LET'S MAKE: SPAGHETTI BRIDGE!

How much spaghetti do you need to hold up a can?

1. Place 2 cans about the length of a piece of spaghetti apart.

2. Balance 10 pieces of spaghetti on the cans like a bridge.

3. Ask yourself: Can the spaghetti bridge hold up the third can? Do you need more or less spaghetti to hold up the can? If you think you need more, add more. If you think you need less, take some spaghetti away.

4. Test it! Carefully **place** the can on top. Did your bridge hold up the can? If not, **keep** trying until you have just the right amount of spaghetti.

LET'S ENGINEER!

The MotMots love to bird-watch, but no birds live nearby.

How can the MotMots attract birds to their neighborhood?

Think about what birds like. Then **build** something that birds will want to visit.

PROJECT 6: DONE!
Get your sticker!

Addition

Circle the hands that make **5**. Then fill in the missing numbers in the number bond.

(1) (4)

5

Circle the hands that make **3**. Then fill in the missing numbers in the number bond.

( ) ( )

3

Circle the hands that make **8**. Then fill in the missing numbers in the number bond.

( ) ( )

8

Circle the hands that make **10**. Then fill in the missing numbers in the number bond.

( ) ( )

10

Add by using the number path. Draw where the animal will be next.

A kangaroo is on 1 and takes 2 steps. Where will he land? Write the number.

A grasshopper is on 5 and takes 3 steps. Where will she land? Write the number.

A rabbit is on 7 and takes 2 steps. Where will he land? Write the number.

A frog is on 9 and takes 1 step. Where will she land? Write the number.

Count the objects in each group. Then fill in the number sentence.

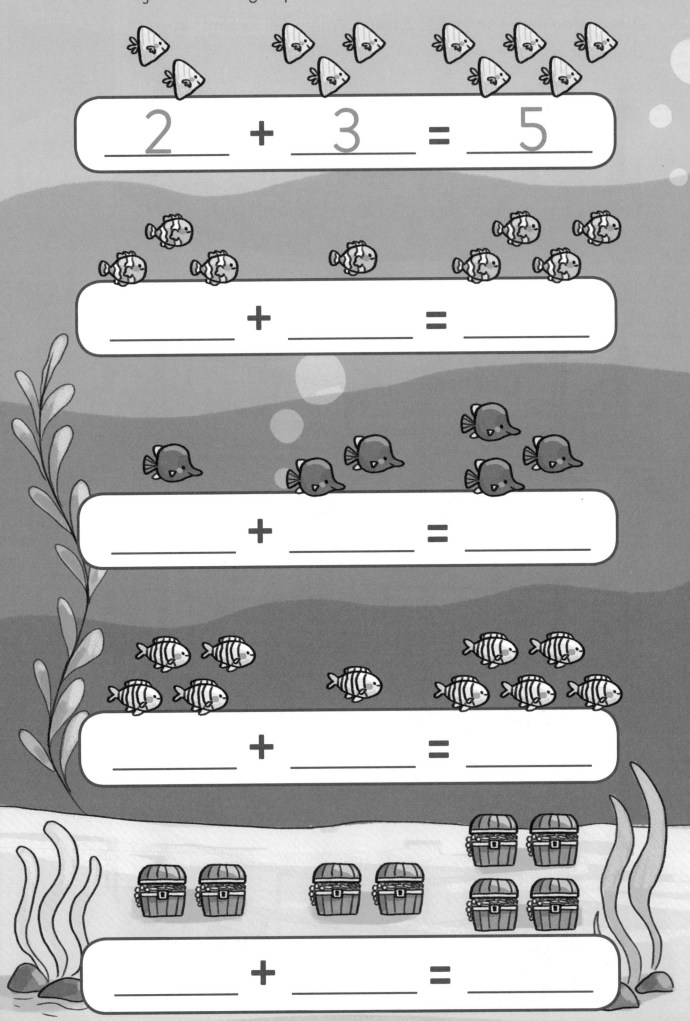

__2__ + __3__ = __5__

____ + ____ = ____

____ + ____ = ____

____ + ____ = ____

____ + ____ = ____

Write each picture as a number sentence.

_____ + _____ ---- 2

_____ + _____ ---- _____

_____ + _____ ---- _____

_____ + _____ ---- _____

Do you notice a pattern? What happens when you add 1 to any number?

_____ + _____ ---- _____

Read each word problem aloud. Then draw it. Last, write the number sentence.

Brian found **3 pink seashells** and **1 orange seashell**. He found **4 seashells** altogether.

_____ + _____ = _____

Amelia is making lunch. She makes **3 ham sandwiches** and 2 cheese sandwiches. She has **5 sandwiches** altogether.

_____ + _____ = _____

Callie loves to dig. She has 1 green shovel and **1 blue shovel**. She has **2 shovels** altogether.

_____ + _____ = _____

Frank is flying his kites. He flies **2 purple kites** and 1 green kite. He has **3 kites** altogether.

_____ + _____ = _____

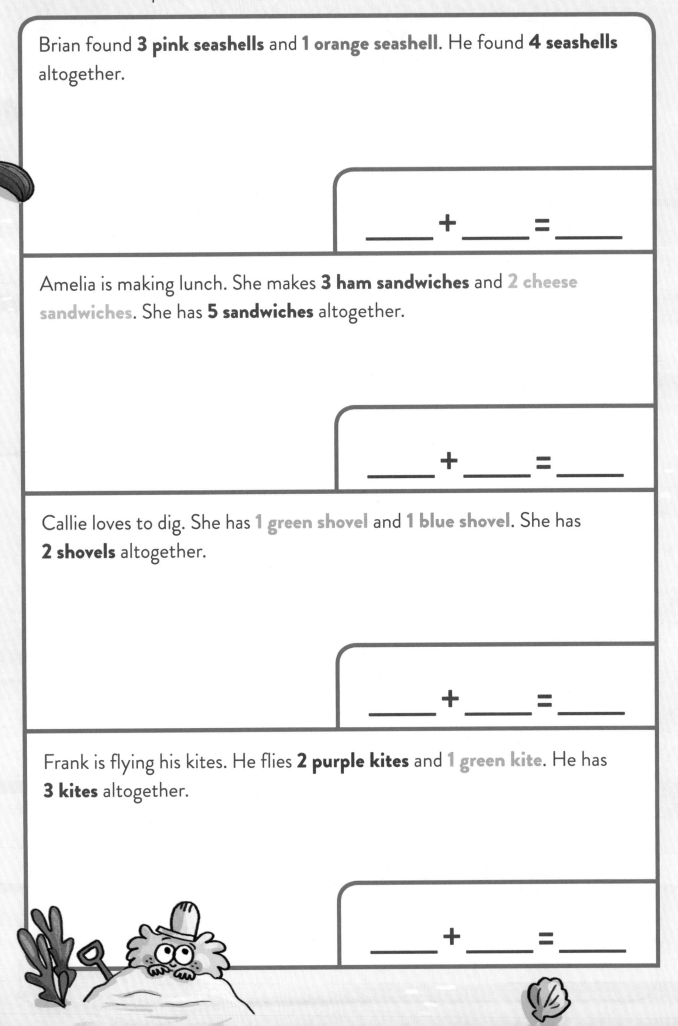

Tell a story to match each number sentence. Then draw it.

6 + 1 = 7

7 + 1 = 8

8 + 1 = 9

9 + 1 = 10

LET'S START! GATHER THESE TOOLS AND MATERIALS.

Paper bag
(lunch bag size)

Markers or crayons

**2 or more toilet paper tubes
or paper towel tubes**

**Poster board or
cardboard**

Tape

Paper cup

10 coins, beads, or marbles
(anything smooth that can roll
or slide easily)

LET'S TINKER!

Create a puppet by adding 1 feature at a time.

Take the paper bag, and draw and use the stickers on page 385 to add 1 feature to it, like a mouth.

Add 1 more feature to your creation, like a nose. **Keep** adding until you get to 10 features. What did your puppet start as? What did your puppet end up becoming? What happened each time you added something?

LET'S MAKE: ADDITION MACHINE!

1. Tape the sides of the paper tubes to the poster board so that they are angled toward each other.

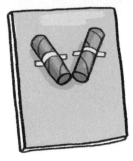

2. Draw a plus sign between the 2 paths.

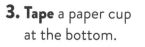
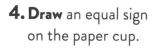

3. Tape a paper cup at the bottom.

4. Draw an equal sign on the paper cup.

5. Now, **count** some coins and drop them into one side. Then **count** some more and drop them into the other. **Predict** how many coins are in the cup.

How many coins ended up in the cup? Was it the number you predicted? Could you get everything into the cup? Keep adjusting your materials until your addition machine works correctly!

LET'S ENGINEER!

There is a new theater being built in Tinker Town! The MotMots want to put on a play for its opening day, but they don't know what should happen in the play. All they know is that they want the story to be about the number 6—their favorite number.

How can the MotMots come up with a story about the number 6?

Make an addition number sentence. Then **think** of a story based on your number sentence, and act it out.

For example, if your number sentence is 3 + 3 = 6, then your story might be: "It's Frank's alligator's birthday! He is turning 6! Brian baked him a cake, but they had only 3 candles. How could they get another 3 candles?"

6
TODAY

PROJECT 7: DONE!
Get your sticker!

Subtraction

Look at each story. Then fill in the number sentence.

3 + 2 = _____

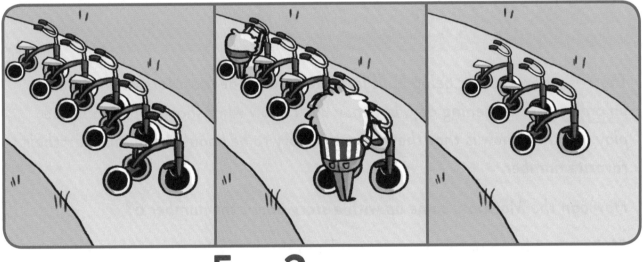

5 − 2 = _____

5 − _____ = _____

Write each picture as a number sentence.

$\underline{4} - \underline{1} = \underline{3}$

$\underline{} - \underline{} = \underline{}$

$\underline{} - \underline{} = \underline{}$

$\underline{} - \underline{} = \underline{}$

Do you notice a pattern? What happens when you subtract 1 from any number?

Draw a line to match each illustration with a number bond.

Try subtracting by using your fingers.
- How many fingers should be up to begin?
- How many fingers should you put down?
- How many fingers are left?

Subtract by using the number path. Draw where the MotMot will be next.

Frank is on 9 and jumps 2 spaces backward. Where will he land? Write the number.

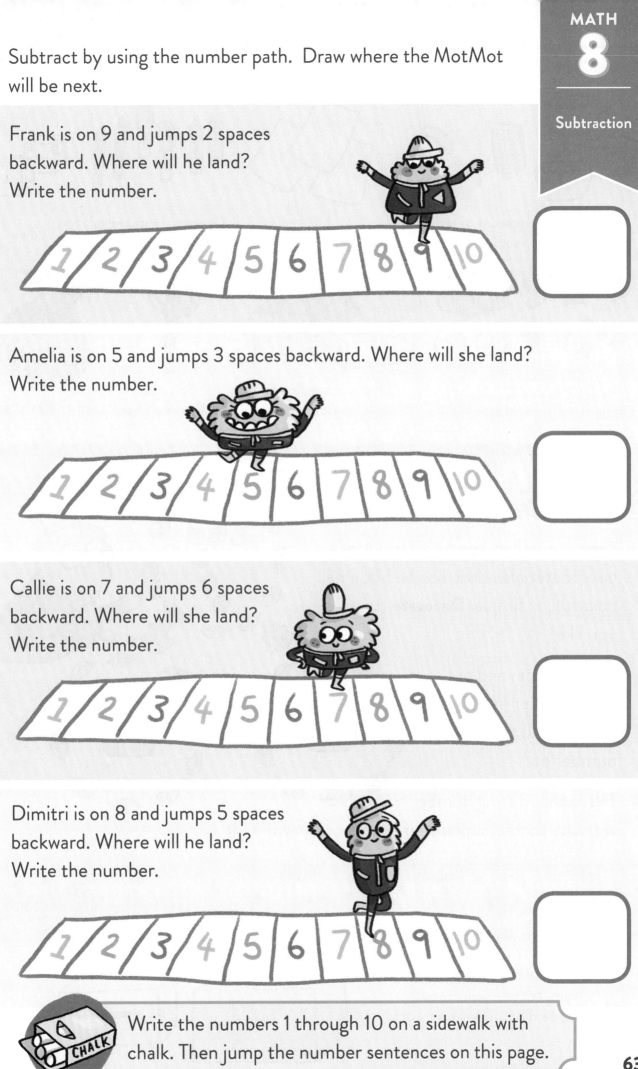

Amelia is on 5 and jumps 3 spaces backward. Where will she land? Write the number.

Callie is on 7 and jumps 6 spaces backward. Where will she land? Write the number.

Dimitri is on 8 and jumps 5 spaces backward. Where will he land? Write the number.

Write the numbers 1 through 10 on a sidewalk with chalk. Then jump the number sentences on this page.

LET'S START!

GATHER THESE TOOLS AND MATERIALS.

3 bowls, 3 long pieces of string, or 3 rubber bands

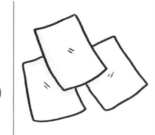

Paper

Crayons, markers, or colored pencils

2 dice

10 snacks like:
pretzels, berries, nuts, pieces of cereal, pieces of popcorn

Empty tissue box or small cardboard box

Scissors
(with an adult's help)

Small trash bag

LET'S TINKER!

Create number-bond circles out of your materials—they can be big, small, colorful, or simple. **Decorate** them as you like!

Roll the dice, and put each number in a circle. What would the missing number be?

Fill in the missing number with the correct amount of snacks or by writing it.

LET'S MAKE: A HUNGRY MONSTER!

1. **Use** the tissue box's hole as a mouth, or cut a hole in your cardboard box to make a mouth.

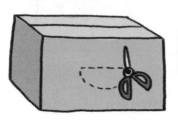
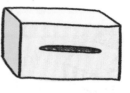

2. Decorate your box with crayons, markers, or colored pencils to make a hungry monster.

3. Your monster is starving! **Put** 1 piece of your snack into your monster's mouth. How many are left? What happens if he eats another piece? **Keep** subtracting and putting snacks into your monster's mouth until all the snacks are gone.

LET'S ENGINEER!

It's garbage day, and the MotMots have to take away all the garbage in the neighborhood.

But how will they know when there's no garbage left?

Count all the pieces of garbage around you now. **Pick** up 1 piece and put it into a trash bag—how many pieces are left? **Pick** up another piece and put it into the trash bag—now how many pieces are left? **Keep** going until you're done. How did you know you were done?

PROJECT 8: DONE!
Get your sticker!

Addition & Subtraction: Unknowns

Look at the picture. Then color the boxes and write the answer.

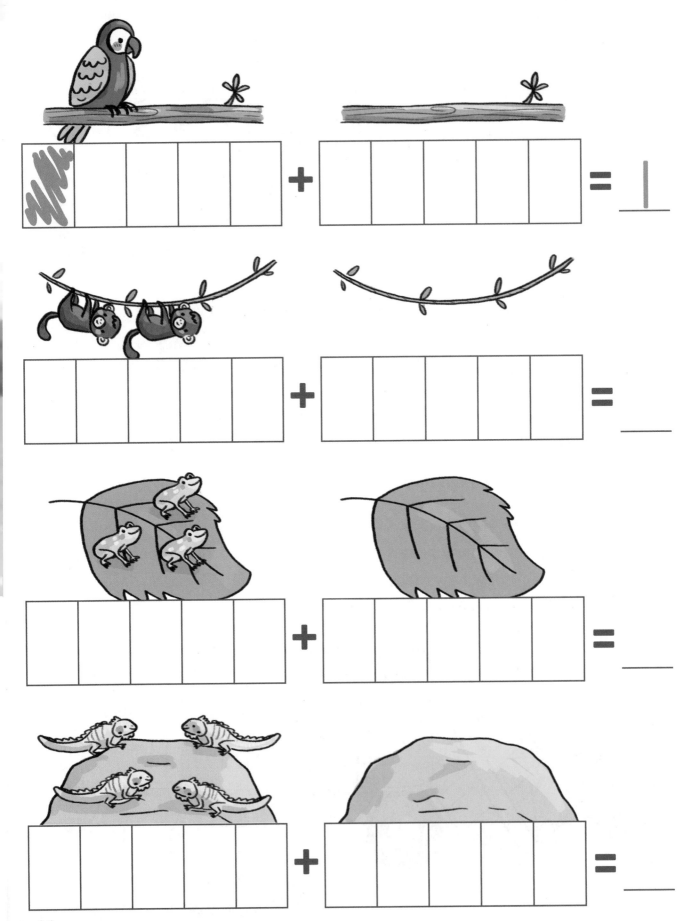

+ = 1

+ = ___

+ = ___

+ = ___

Do you notice a pattern? What happens when you add zero to any number?

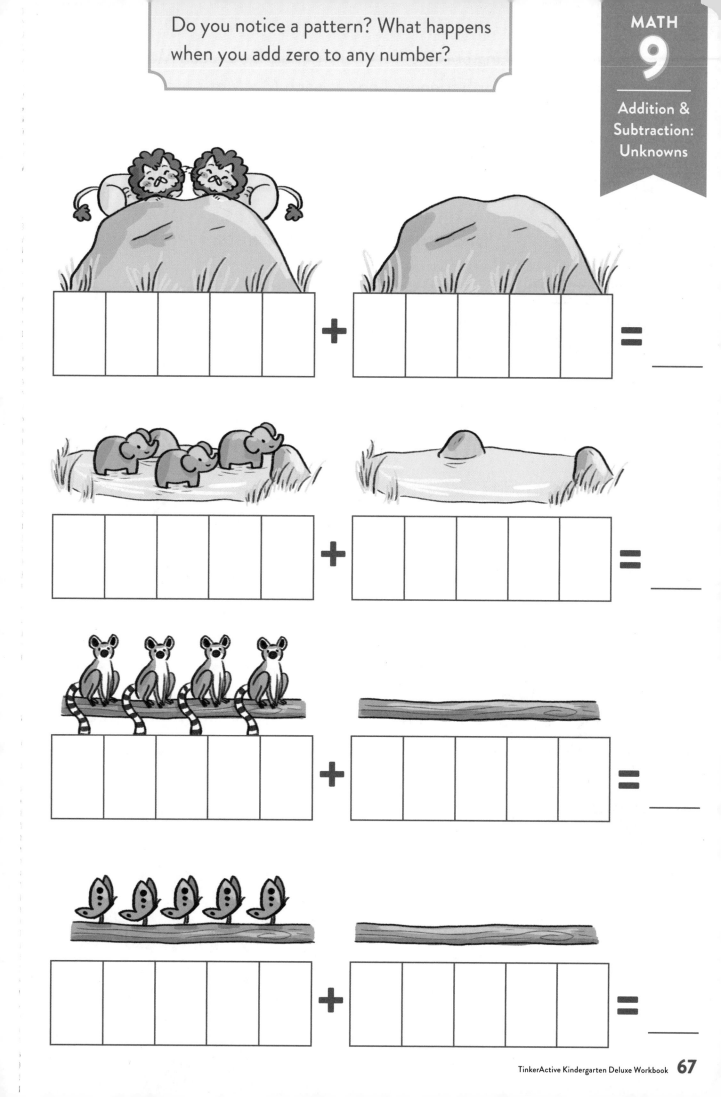

+ = ___

+ = ___

+ = ___

+ = ___

The MotMots are making presents for their friends. Does each MotMot have enough presents for 5 friends? Look at each MotMot's presents. Fill in each sentence, then read it aloud.

Brian made _____ bracelets. He needs to make _____ more to have **5**.

This MotMot made _____ bookmarks. She needs to make _____ more to have **5**.

Callie made _____ painting. She needs to make _____ more to have **5**.

Dimitri made _____ monsters. He needs to make _____ more to have **5**.

Does each MotMot have enough presents for 10 friends? Look at each MotMot's presents. Fill in each sentence, then read it aloud.

Amelia made _____ masks. She needs to make _____ more to have **10**.

Enid made _____ snakes. She needs to make _____ more to have **10**.

Frank made _____ flower vases. He needs to make _____ more to have **10**.

This MotMot made _____ mugs. She needs to make _____ more to have **10**.

Count the number of fingers. Then draw the fingers you need to make 10.

Try raising the same number of fingers as the MotMot.
How many more fingers do you need to raise to have 10?
Another way to find the answer is to ask: How many
fingers do I have left?

Fill in the missing numbers.

$3 + 1 = \boxed{}$

$4 = \boxed{} + 1$

$4 - \boxed{} = 3$

$10 = \boxed{} + 9$

$10 = \boxed{} + 1$

$\boxed{} - 9 = 1$

$\boxed{} + 4 = 10$

$10 - \boxed{} = 4$

$10 = 6 + \boxed{}$

$5 + \boxed{} = 7$

$7 - \boxed{} = 2$

$2 = \boxed{} - 5$

Write your own number sentence. Then tell a story to match your number sentence, and draw it.

$10 = \underline{} + \underline{}$

LET'S START!

Tongs or clothespin

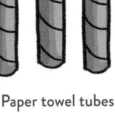

Paper towel tubes

Sticks

Newspaper

Crayons or markers

Scissors
(with an adult's help)

Glue, tape, pipe cleaner, or string

Construction paper

LET'S TINKER!

Play with each of your objects to see how they move. Does the object roll, lie flat, fold, slide, drip, or grab?

Find 10 unique ways that your materials can move. How does the motion happen?

Find 10 unique ways you move! How do your body parts—fingers, toes, arms, and legs—create motion?

LET'S MAKE: A MOTMOT!

1. **Choose** your favorite MotMot.
2. **Find** an object that is shaped like your favorite MotMot's body.
3. **Use** your materials to make 2 legs, 2 arms, and a hat.
4. **Put** the objects together.

5. **Add** stickers from page 385 to decorate your MotMot.

6. How many objects did you use in all? **Count** the number of objects you used in total.

LET'S ENGINEER!

It's Friendship Day in Tinker Town! Dimitri wants to send something to his 10 closest buddies. But he only has money to buy 2 cards.

If Dimitri only has 2 cards, how many friends won't get anything? What can he do for his remaining friends instead?

Think of something else Dimitri can send or make for the remaining friends. Then **create** something for the same number of your own friends.

PROJECT 9: DONE!
Get your sticker!

Place Value

Circle 10 vegetables in each group. How many vegetables are left over? Fill in the missing number, and read it aloud.

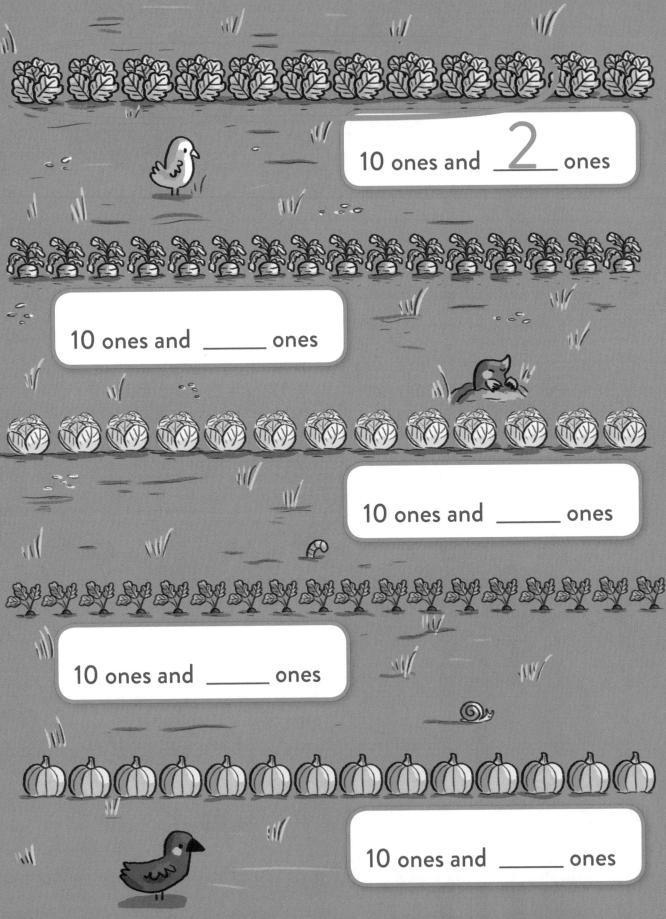

10 ones and __2__ ones

10 ones and _____ ones

10 ones and _____ ones

10 ones and _____ ones

10 ones and _____ ones

Draw flowers to match each amount.

10 ones and 4 ones

10 ones and 5 ones

10 ones and 1 one

10 ones and 7 ones

10 ones and 9 ones

Read the number on the left aloud. Then draw a line to match it with the correct amount on the right. Last, circle the amount that is missing.

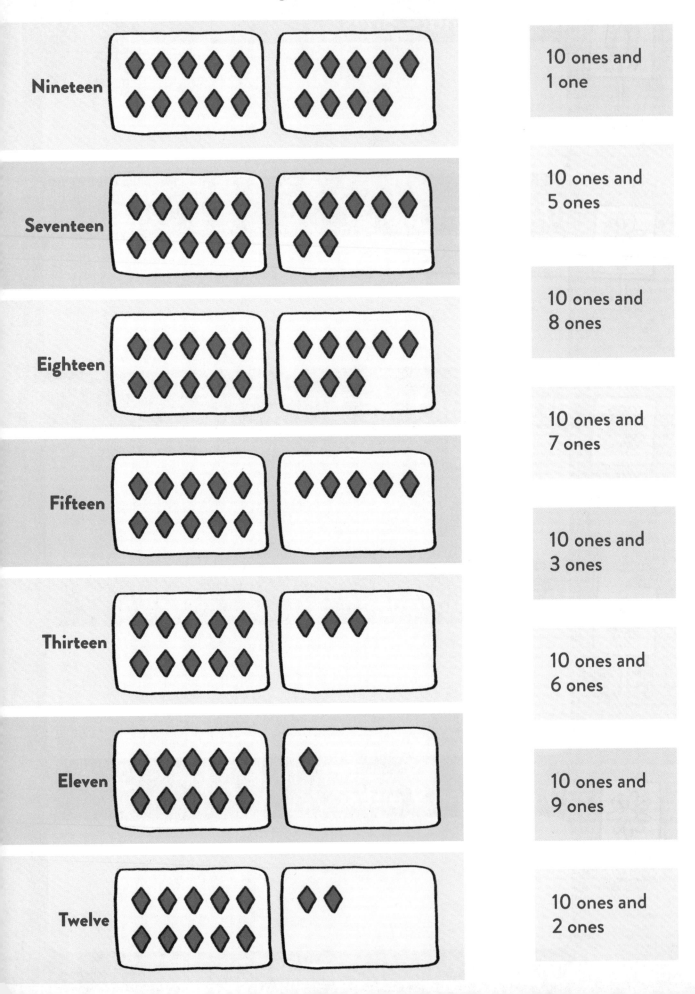

Nineteen

Seventeen

Eighteen

Fifteen

Thirteen

Eleven

Twelve

10 ones and
1 one

10 ones and
5 ones

10 ones and
8 ones

10 ones and
7 ones

10 ones and
3 ones

10 ones and
6 ones

10 ones and
9 ones

10 ones and
2 ones

Read each word problem aloud. Fill in the
number sentence and solve.

10 MotMots are playing Duck, Duck, Goose, and 2 more want to
join the game. How many MotMots want to play altogether?

10 ones + _____ ones = _____

10 MotMots are playing Red Rover, and 4 more want to join the game.
How many MotMots want to play altogether?

10 ones + _____ ones = _____

10 MotMots are playing Mother May I, and 1 more wants to join the game.
How many MotMots want to play altogether?

10 ones + _____ one = _____

10 MotMots are playing Simon Says, and 3 more want to join the game.
How many MotMots want to play altogether?

10 ones + _____ ones = _____

The MotMots are going on a scavenger hunt! Help them by writing the correct amount of each object they need. Then find the correct amount of each object in their neighborhood and circle it.

10 ones + 2 ones = ☐ squirrels

10 ones + 7 ones = ☐ newspapers

10 ones + 8 ones = ☐ dogs

10 ones + 3 ones = ☐ leaves

10 ones + 9 ones = ☐ birds

10 ones + 6 ones = ☐ mailboxes

10 ones + 5 ones = ☐ cars

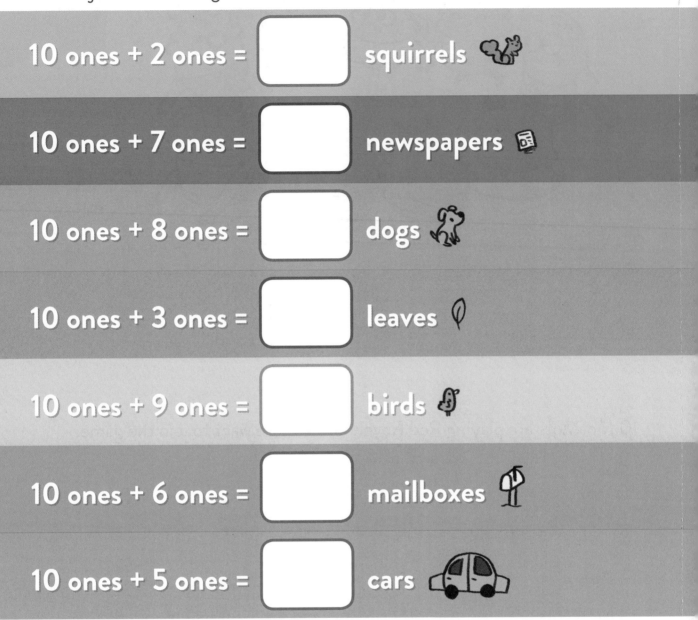

Use this list for your own scavenger hunt! Tear this page out of the book. Check each item off as you find it on your walk. Can you find them all?

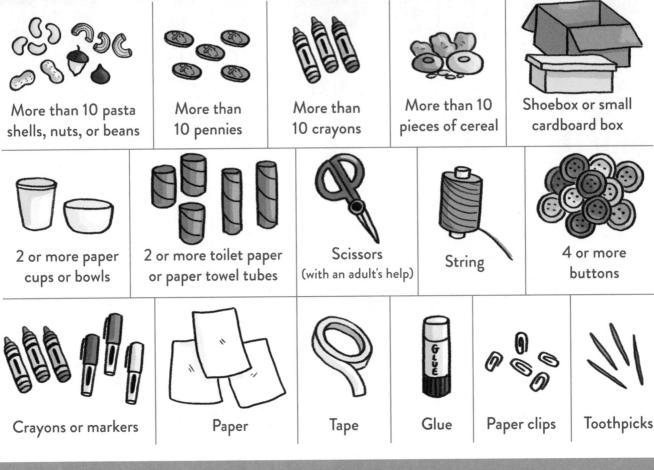

| More than 10 pasta shells, nuts, or beans | More than 10 pennies | More than 10 crayons | More than 10 pieces of cereal | Shoebox or small cardboard box |

| 2 or more paper cups or bowls | 2 or more toilet paper or paper towel tubes | Scissors (with an adult's help) | String | 4 or more buttons |

| Crayons or markers | Paper | Tape | Glue | Paper clips | Toothpicks |

LET'S TINKER!

Put your pasta shells, pennies, crayons, and cereal in the box and shake them up.

Dump them out and separate the objects into groups. How many tens and ones are in each group?

Arrange the groups of 10 into different shapes. Which shape makes it easiest to see 10 ones? Can you arrange the objects in other shapes that make it even easier to count 10 ones?

LET'S MAKE: HAUL TRUCK!

Look at a nearby street or road. What vehicles carry lots of people or objects?

Make a vehicle that can carry lots of things.

Think about how you can make it move. Can you push it, pull it, or roll it?

When your vehicle is ready, **put** objects inside it. Then **count** the objects you put inside it.

LET'S ENGINEER!

A new park is opening in Tinker Town, and there's a contest for who can design the best playground. Brian and Enid are both competing. Lots and lots of MotMots will want to play there, so they need to think of fun things that can hold more than 10 MotMots.

How can more than 10 MotMots play safely together at the playground at the same time?

Design a playground for lots of MotMots to enjoy. **Draw** a poster showing what you would put in the playground.

PROJECT 10: DONE!
Get your sticker!

Comparing Measurements

Circle the buildings that are the same height. Then draw another building that is the same height.

Circle the taller building. Then draw an even taller building.

Circle the shorter building. Then draw an even shorter building.

Look around. What is taller than you? What is shorter than you? What is the same height as you? Stand next to different objects to find out!

Circle the buses that are the same length. Then draw another bus that is the same length.

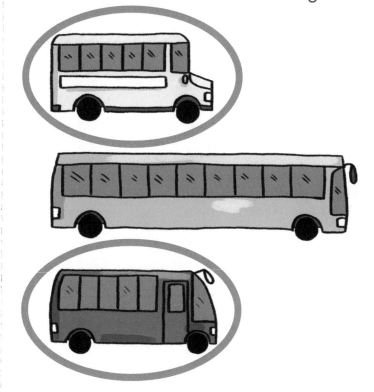

Circle the longer truck. Then draw an even longer truck.

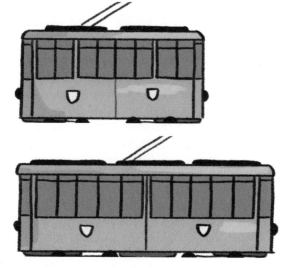

Circle the shorter trolley. Then draw an even shorter trolley.

Lay your arm next to different objects! What is longer than your arm? What is shorter? What is the same length?

Circle the cats that are the same weight. Then draw another cat that is the same weight.

Circle the heavier turtle. Then draw an even heavier turtle.

Circle the lighter dog. Then draw an even lighter dog.

Circle the object that has more milk. Then draw something that has even more milk.

Circle the object that has less soup. Then draw something that has even less soup.

Circle the objects that hold the same amount of water. Then draw another object that holds the same amount of water.

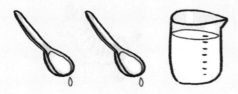

Circle the spoon that holds more soup. Then draw another spoon that holds even more soup.

Circle the bottle that holds less juice. Then draw another bottle that holds even less juice.

The next time you're at the dinner table, look around. Who has more to drink? Who has less? Who has the same amount as you? Try putting your glasses next to each other to find out.

Look at the pictures. Then fill in the sentences with words from the box above. Last, read each sentence aloud.

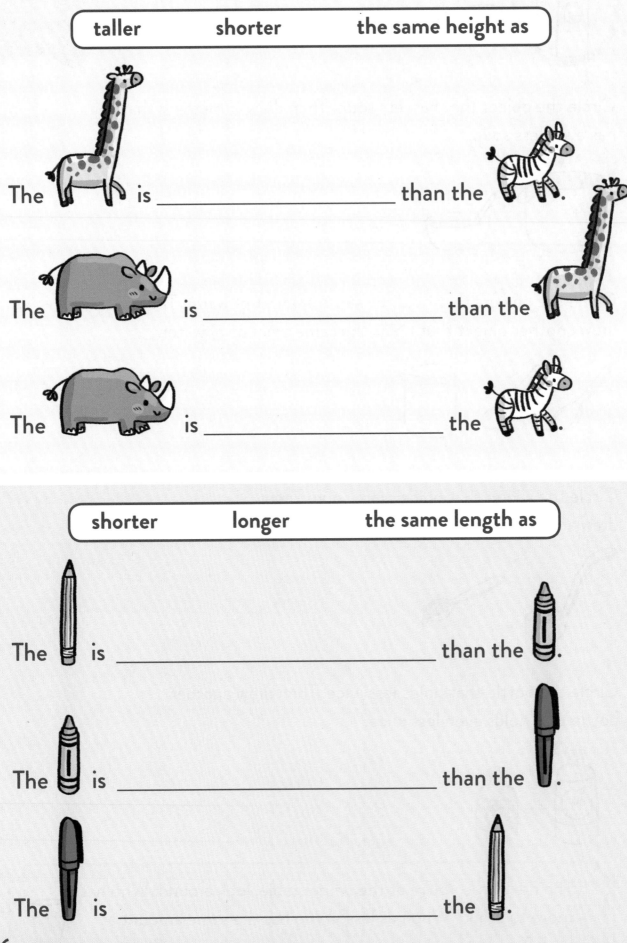

taller   shorter   the same height as

The ___ is _____ than the ___.

The ___ is _____ than the ___.

The ___ is _____ the ___.

shorter   longer   the same length as

The ___ is _____ than the ___.

The ___ is _____ than the ___.

The ___ is _____ the ___.

heavier   lighter   the same weight as

The 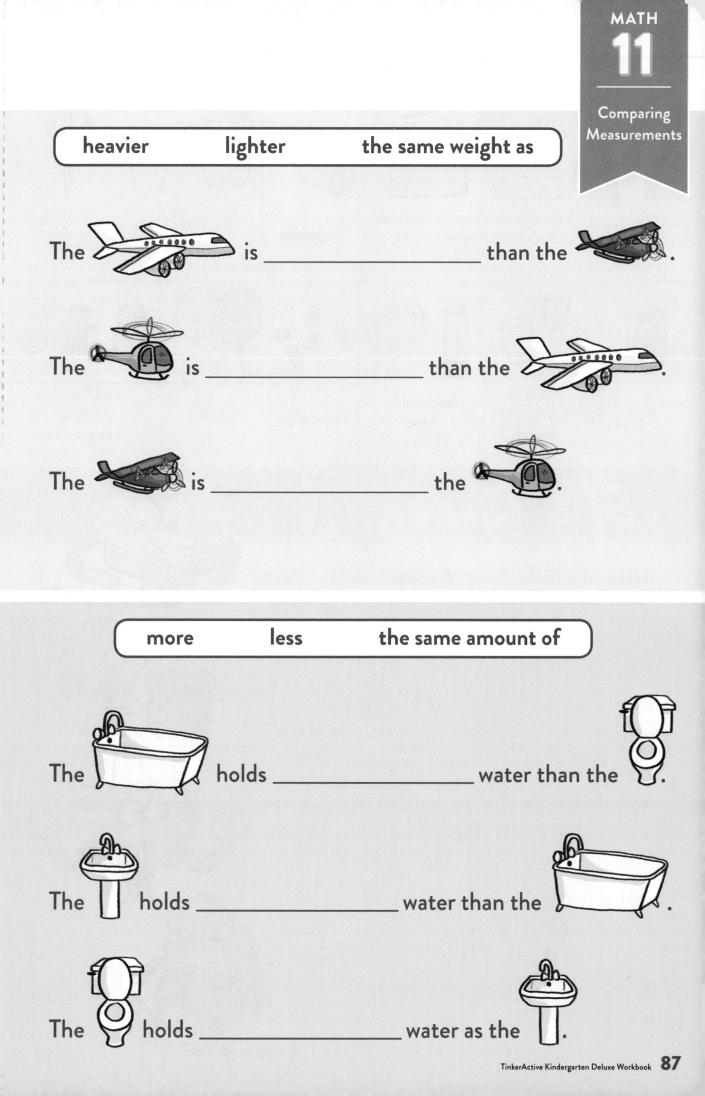 is _____ than the .

The is _____ than the .

The is _____ the .

more   less   the same amount of

The holds _____ water than the .

The holds _____ water than the .

The holds _____ water as the .

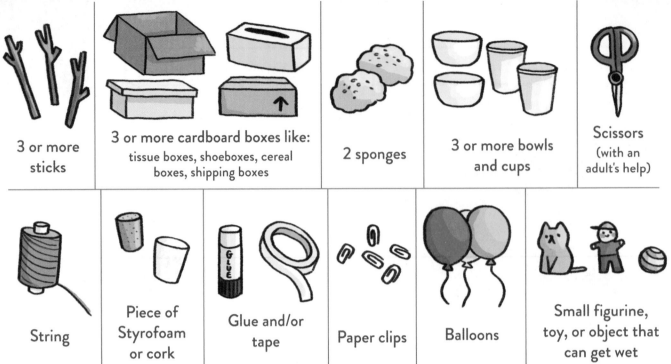

3 or more sticks

3 or more cardboard boxes like: tissue boxes, shoeboxes, cereal boxes, shipping boxes

2 sponges

3 or more bowls and cups

Scissors (with an adult's help)

String

Piece of Styrofoam or cork

Glue and/or tape

Paper clips

Balloons

Small figurine, toy, or object that can get wet

LET'S TINKER!

Gather the sticks. Are they equal in length? If not, which is longest and which is shortest? **Lay** them on the ground to show which is longest and which is shortest.

Get the boxes. Are they equal in height? If not, which is tallest and which is shortest? **Stand** them up to show which is tallest and which is shortest.

Grab the sponges. Is one heavier or lighter, or are they equal in weight? **Dip** 1 sponge into a bowl of water. Did the weight change? Why or why not?

Gather the bowls and cups. Can they hold the same amount? If not, which holds the most and which holds the least? **Fill** them up with water to show which holds the most and which holds the least.

LET'S MAKE: FISHING ROD!

Some fish swim near the surface of the water, and some fish swim deeper. **Make** a fishing rod that can catch fish in just the right place!

To catch a fish that swims near the top of the water, you need a bobber on your string—that's something light that floats.

To catch a fish that swims deeper, you need a sinker on your string—that's something heavy that sinks.

Build a fishing pole and try different weights at the end of your "line" or string. **Test** it out in a large deep bowl of water or your tub or kitchen sink.

LET'S ENGINEER!

A flock of ducks has landed near Tinker Town, and the MotMots want to welcome them ashore.

How can the MotMots reach the ducks?

Design a bridge that is long but can also stand over water. **Use** your kitchen sink, bathroom sink, or tub as a mini version of the lake.

Draw a design for your bridge first. Then **choose** materials to build it with.

Last, **put** your bridge on the edge of the sink or tub. Does it stand up? Is it strong enough to hold a small figurine or toy?

Try putting your toy in different places on the bridge. **Keep** trying to improve your bridge.

PROJECT 11: DONE!
Get your sticker!

Units of Measurement

How long is each row of blocks? Count and write the number of blocks.

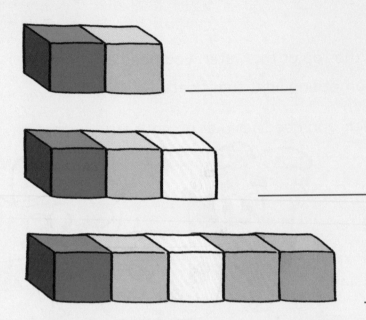

_____

_____

_____

How long is each toy? Color the blocks that are below the toy—from end to end. Then count and write the number of blocks.

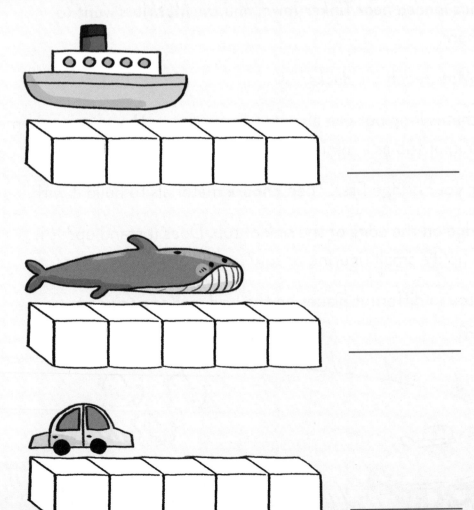

_____

_____

_____

How tall is each tower of blocks? Count and write the number of blocks.

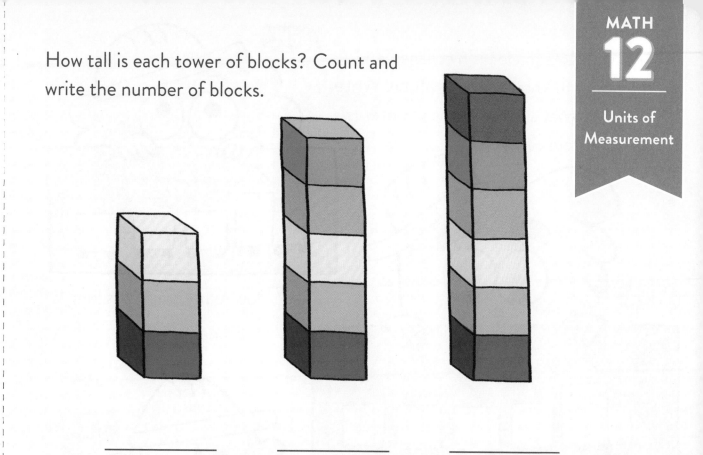

_____   _____   _____

How tall is each toy? Color the blocks that are next to the toy—from its toes to its head. Then count and write the number of blocks.

_____   _____

_____

The MotMots made train collages, and they want to know whose is whose. Write each MotMot's name so that 1 letter is on each train car.

Enid

How many train cars long is Enid's name? _____

Brian

How many train cars long is Brian's name? _____

Frank

How many train cars long is Frank's name? _____

Dimitri

How many train cars long is Dimitri's name? _____

Make your own train collage and write your name on it. How many train cars long is your name?

_____

Are any of the names the same length? If so, circle them.

Is there one name that is the longest? If so, write an ✗ next to it.

Is there one name that is the shortest? If so, write a ✔ next to it.

The MotMots were visiting the library. They asked the librarian for a map of their favorite place—the playground! But someone had already borrowed it. So the MotMots decided to make their own while the librarian described the map.

Listen carefully to the description and draw your own map of the playground.

In the middle of Tinker Town's playground is a tower as tall as your pointer finger.

Next to the tower is a bridge. The bridge is as long as 2 thumbs, and each side is as tall as 1 thumb.

On the other side of the tower is a tree that is taller than 2 pinkie fingers.

Next to the tree is a seesaw that is as long as 1 pinkie finger.

Last, draw some MotMots playing. They should be smaller than your pinkie finger.

Cut out the ribbon at the bottom of the page. Then compare the ribbon with each object to see which is taller. Circle the objects that are taller than the ribbon.

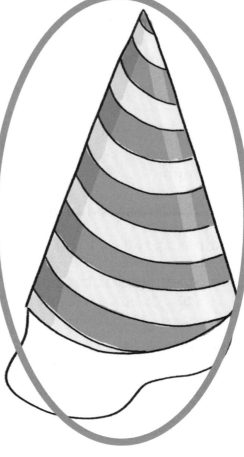

Compare the ribbon with each object to see which is longer.
Circle the objects that are longer than the ribbon.

20 or more paper clips

Markers and crayons

Toilet paper

2 Toys

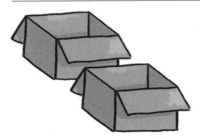

2 or more empty cardboard, pasta, or cereal boxes

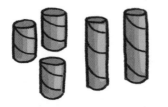

4 or more toilet paper tubes or paper towel tubes

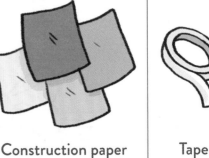

Construction paper

Tape

LET'S TINKER!

Measure furniture around your home using different objects, such as paper clips, crayons, or toilet paper. How long is your table in crayons? What about in toilet paper squares or paper clips? What other materials might be good for measuring objects?

LET'S MAKE: THE PERFECT HOME!

1. **Choose** two different toys.

2. **Build** homes for each using cardboard boxes or cereal boxes. Perhaps a doghouse for a plush puppy, a garage for your truck, a space station for your Martian, or a magical barn for your unicorn!

   How did you know how tall the home should be? How did you know how long it should be?

3. **Decorate** your toys' new homes.

LET'S ENGINEER!

Enid is not very tall. She has a hard time reaching all the yummy snacks on the kitchen counter.

How can you help her get to the snacks?

Pretend your favorite doll or plush animal is Enid. What materials are strong enough and safe for your doll to stand, sit, or climb on?

Build something that is strong enough to stand on and tall enough for your doll to reach your kitchen counter.

PROJECT 12: DONE!
Get your sticker!

Naming Shapes

Color the shapes that have sides in blue. Color the shapes that have no sides in red.

Look at the picture above and answer each question.

How many shapes have 4 sides? _____

How many shapes have 3 sides? _____

How many shapes have 6 sides? _____

How many shapes have no sides? _____

Trace each shape. Then read the name aloud and answer each question.

side   corner

What is my name? <u>Square</u>

How many sides do I have? _____

How many corners do I have? <u>4</u>

What is my name? <u>Rectangle</u>

How many sides do I have? _____

How many corners do I have? _____

What is my name? <u>Triangle</u>

How many sides do I have? _____

How many corners do I have? _____

What is my name? <u>Hexagon</u>

How many sides do I have? _____

How many corners do I have? _____

What is my name? <u>Circle</u>

How many sides do I have? _____

How many corners do I have? _____

Read the story aloud. Then color the shapes according to the key.

Every week, the MotMots throw a shape parade!
They march through town to celebrate their favorite shapes.
Frank loves triangles.
Brian likes rectangles.
Enid's favorite shape is the circle.
Dimitri loves hexagons,
and Amelia likes squares.
They love their shapes so much,
they play and sing for the whole world to hear!

COLOR KEY

Circle: Yellow

Rectangle: Blue

Triangle: Green

Hexagon: Orange

Square: Pink

If you put shapes together, you can make something new!
Draw a line to match the groups of shapes with the new shape.

With an adult's help, cut out the shapes on the previous page and use the pieces to make each shape below. Then fill in each sentence.

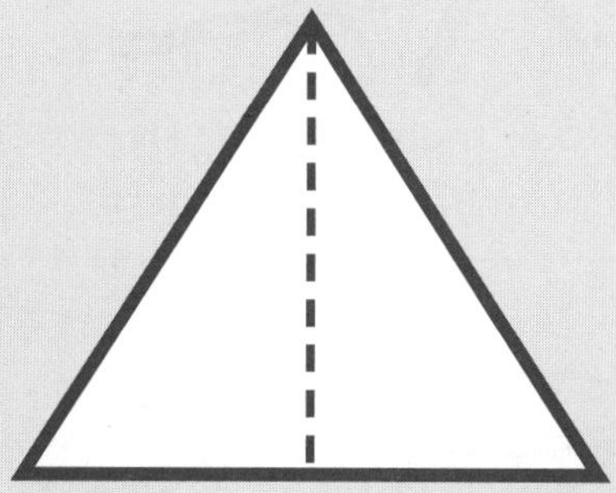

I made a triangle out of

_____.

I made a square out of

_____.

I made a square out of

_____.

I made a rectangle out of

_____.

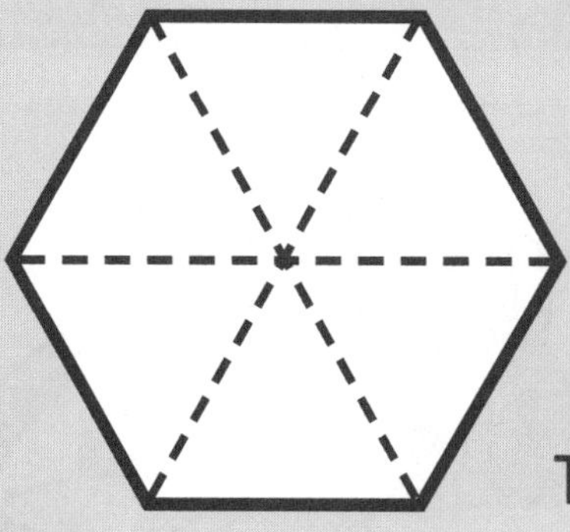

I made a hexagon out of

_____.

The only shape I didn't use was a _____.

LET'S START!

GATHER THESE TOOLS AND MATERIALS.

Old wire hangers

6 or more twigs or branches

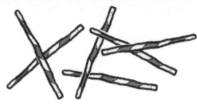

6 or more drinking straws and/or pipe cleaners

Bubble solution, or $\frac{2}{3}$ cup liquid dish soap and 1 gallon water

(optional: 2 or 3 tablespoons of glycerin with an adult's help)

Tray or bucket

Tape

LET'S TINKER!

Bend the wire hanger, twigs, and straws. What do you notice? Are some materials easier to bend than others?

Create some shapes by bending these materials. Are some shapes easier or harder to make? Why or why not? Can you combine shapes to make a picture?

LET'S MAKE: BUBBLE WANDS!

1. Twist the hangers into different shapes—make sure the ends of the wire touch.

2. With the help of an adult, **pour** the bubble solution—or your dish soap and water solution—into a tray or bucket.

3. Lower your wand into the bubble solution, pull it out gently, and blow.

What happens? Are your bubbles different with differently shaped wands? Why or why not?

LET'S ENGINEER!

The MotMots love to play basketball, but they don't have a bouncing ball or a hoop.

How can the MotMots play a game like basketball anyway?

Design a game that is like basketball using only the materials you have. What could replace the ball? What can you make into a hoop? How will the players move the "ball"?

PROJECT 13: DONE!
Get your sticker!

Spatial Reasoning

The MotMots are on safari! Tell them where each animal is by tracing the words and reading each sentence aloud.

A bird is _above_ the tree.

The zebras are _behind_ the trees.

The lions are _beside_ the watering hole.

The lion cub is _in_ its mother's mouth.

The giraffe is _next to_ the watering hole.

A bird is _on_ the hippo.

The baby elephant is _below_ his mother.

The snake is _beside_ the rocks.

The warthogs are _in front of_ the bush.

The meerkat is _next to_ the bush.

The mouse is _in front of_ the anthill.

The deer is _behind_ the anthill.

Circle the word that completes each sentence. Then read the sentence aloud.

Callie is

beside   **below**

the umbrella.

Brian is

next to   **on**

a worm.

Amelia is

in front of   **behind**

a frog.

Dimitri is

in front of   **below**

the flowers.

Frank is

below   **on**

the rock.

Frank is

in   **above**

the puddle.

Enid made a rainy-day collage! Look at the collage and complete each sentence.

| circle | rectangle | hexagon | triangle |

I have **3 sides**, and I am above Enid. I am a _____.

I have **4 sides**, and I am in front of the trees. I am a _____.

I have **no sides**, and I am behind the clouds. I am a _____.

I have **6 sides**, and I am next to the bench. I am a _____.

Create a model of space! With an adult's help, cut out the objects below and paste them on the following page according to the directions.

Paste the Sun beside Mercury.

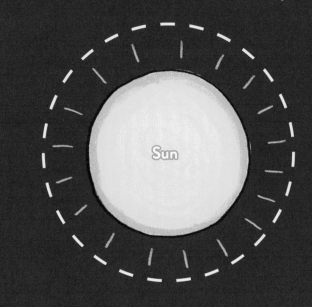

Paste Neptune next to Uranus.

Paste Saturn's ring on Saturn.

Paste the space shuttle and astronaut wherever you like.

Paste the stars above and below the planets.

Fill in the sentences:

I pasted the space shuttle _____

_____.

I pasted the astronaut _____

_____.

Mercury

Venus

Earth

Mars

Jupiter

Saturn

Uranus

LET'S START!

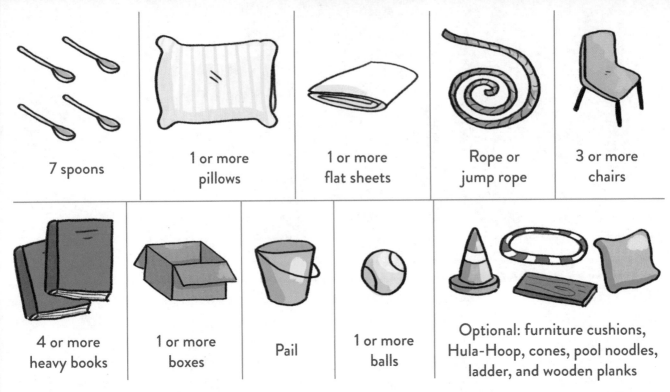

7 spoons

1 or more pillows

1 or more flat sheets

Rope or jump rope

3 or more chairs

4 or more heavy books

1 or more boxes

Pail

1 or more balls

Optional: furniture cushions, Hula-Hoop, cones, pool noodles, ladder, and wooden planks

LET'S TINKER!

Hide 7 spoons throughout your home.

Ask an adult, sibling, or friend to go on a spoon hunt!

Describe your hiding spots using the following: above, below, beside, in front of, behind, on, and in.

1. **Make** an obstacle course race. **Include** the following activities:

   - Jumping above something.
   - Crawling below something.
   - Walking on something.
   - Throwing a ball into something.
   - Weaving in front of and behind something.

2. **Ask** a friend to race with you.

LET'S ENGINEER!

The MotMots want to build a fort that keeps them safe from an invasion.

How can they build something that keeps the MotMots inside and the invaders outside?

Design a fort that's large enough to go inside. Which materials can make a wall? How can the materials be combined to keep your walls up? How will you stop invaders far from the entrance?

PROJECT 14: DONE!
Get your sticker!

Is each shape 2-dimensional or 3-dimensional? Color the flat, 2-dimensional shapes in red. Color the solid, 3-dimensional shapes in blue.

Circle the object that has the same face or surface as the 2-dimensional shape.

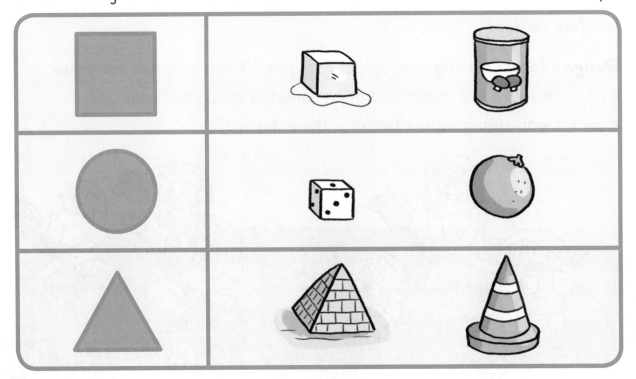

Trace each shape. Then read the name aloud, and answer each question.

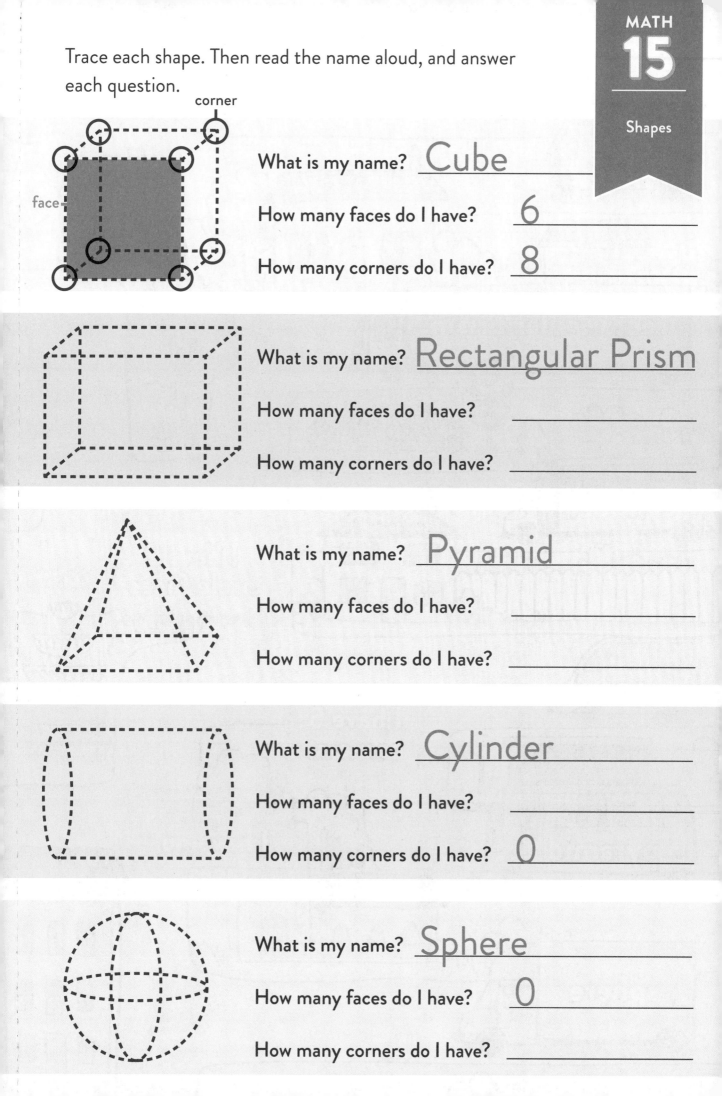

corner

face

What is my name? _Cube_

How many faces do I have? _6_

How many corners do I have? _8_

What is my name? _Rectangular Prism_

How many faces do I have? _____

How many corners do I have? _____

What is my name? _Pyramid_

How many faces do I have? _____

How many corners do I have? _____

What is my name? _Cylinder_

How many faces do I have? _____

How many corners do I have? _0_

What is my name? _Sphere_

How many faces do I have? _0_

How many corners do I have? _____

Match each name to its shape by drawing a line through the maze. If you pass a sign, read it aloud for a hint.

Go on a shape scavenger hunt! Look at each shape and trace the name.
Then find objects in your home that are or have the same shapes.
Draw each object below.

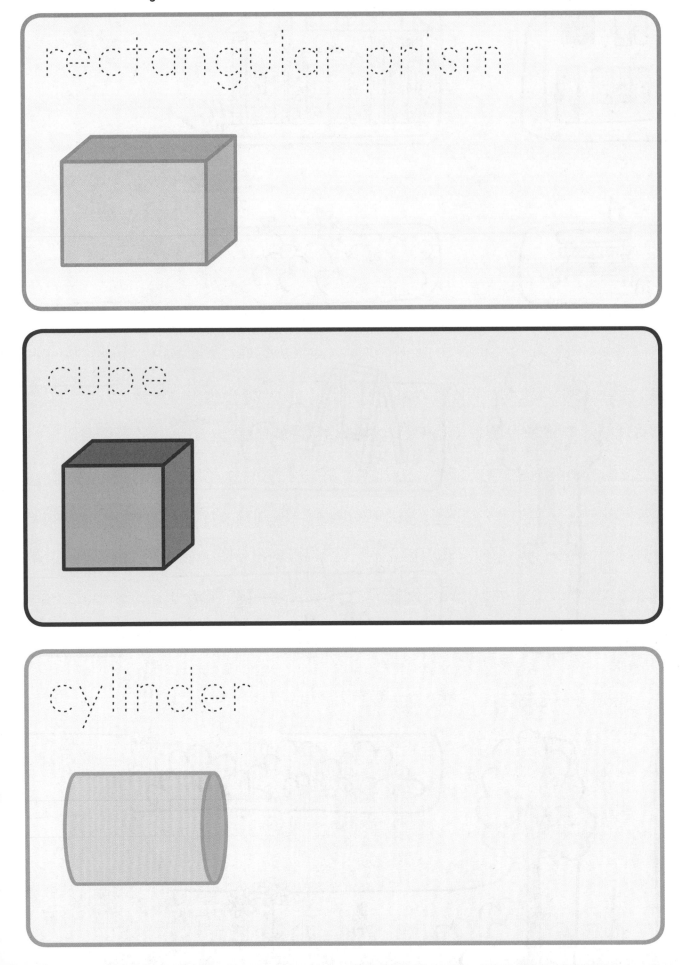

rectangular prism

cube

cylinder

sphere

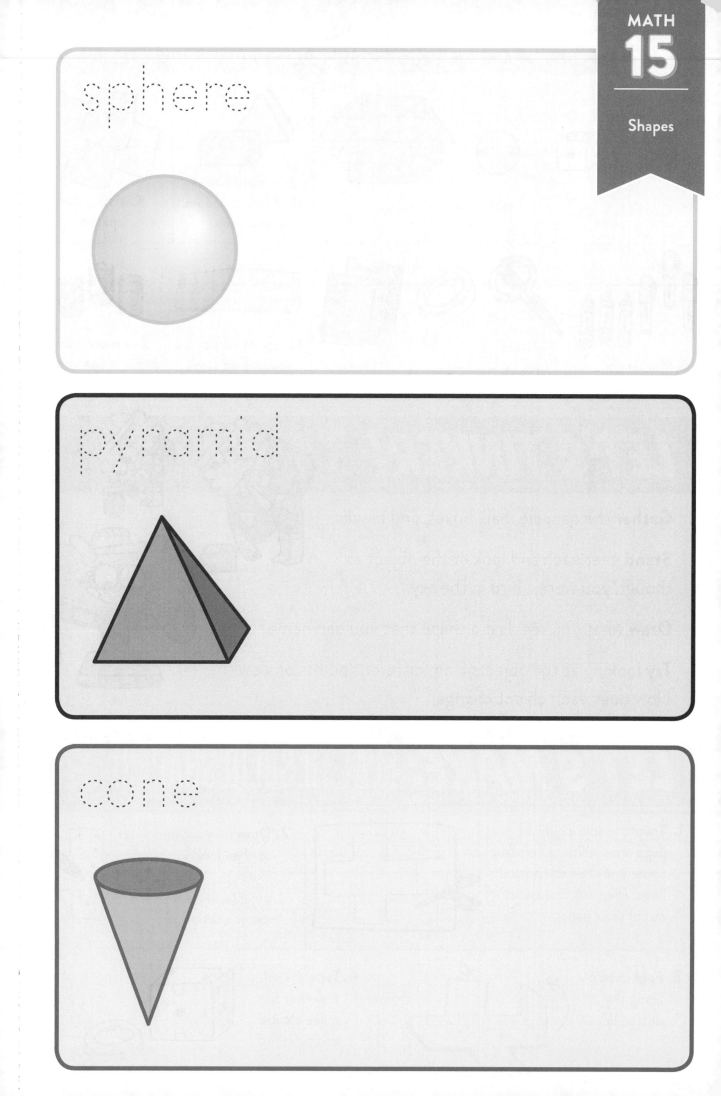

pyramid

cone

LET'S START! GATHER THESE TOOLS AND MATERIALS.

Can	Die	Ball	Boxes	2 or more blocks of different shapes and sizes	Construction paper
Markers or crayons	Scissors (with an adult's help)	Tape	Heavy books	1 piece of cardboard roughly an arm's length long	2 or more toilet paper tubes and/or paper towel tubes

LET'S TINKER!

Gather the can, die, ball, boxes, and blocks.

Stand over each and look at the object as though you were a bird in the sky.

Draw what you see. Is it a shape that you can name?

Try looking at the objects from different points of view. How does each object change?

LET'S MAKE: FLAT TO SOLID SHAPES!

1. **Trace** the shapes on the next page onto white or construction paper and draw the dotted lines. Then **cut** the shapes out of your paper.

2. **Draw** on your templates so they look like real objects, like a die or a drum!

3. **Fold** inward along the dotted lines.

4. **Tape** the sides together to make a cube and cylinder.

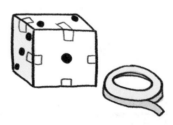

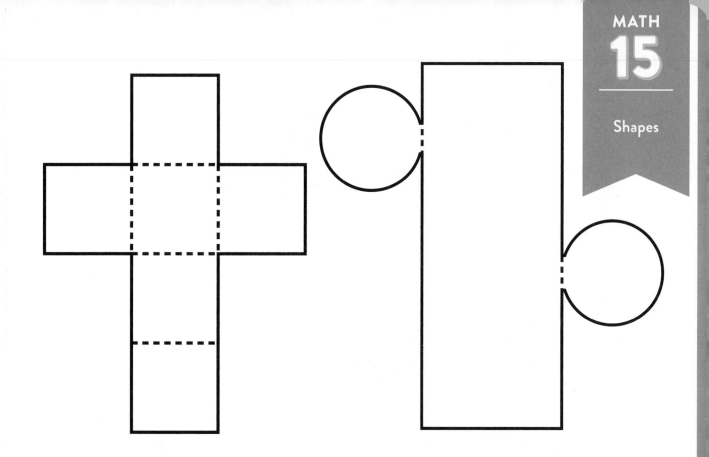

LET'S ENGINEER!

Just outside Tinker Town is a big hill where all the MotMots go sledding. Some MotMots love to go fast, and some love to go slow. Some love to go straight, and some love to turn and wind downhill. But the last time they went sledding they broke their sled.

How can the MotMots build sleds that go down a hill fast, slow, straight, and zigzag?

Use a few books piled up and a piece of cardboard to make a ramp.

Think about the way different shapes go downhill. Are some shapes faster or slower? Will some shapes go straight or zigzag?

PROJECT 15: DONE!
Get your sticker!

ANSWER KEY

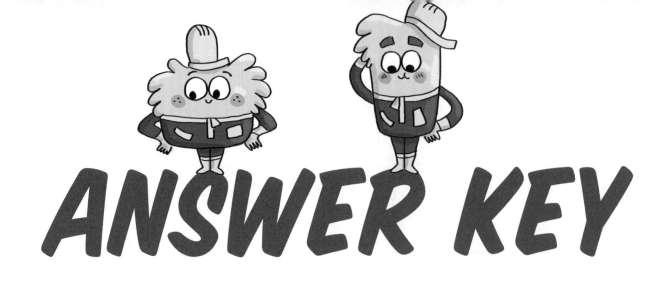

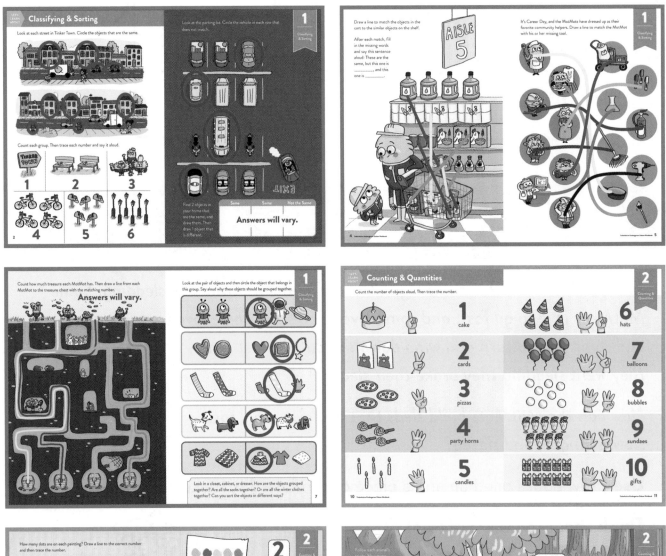

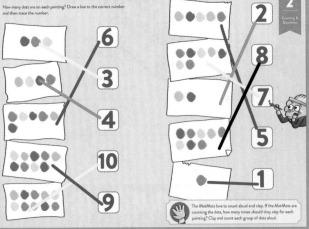

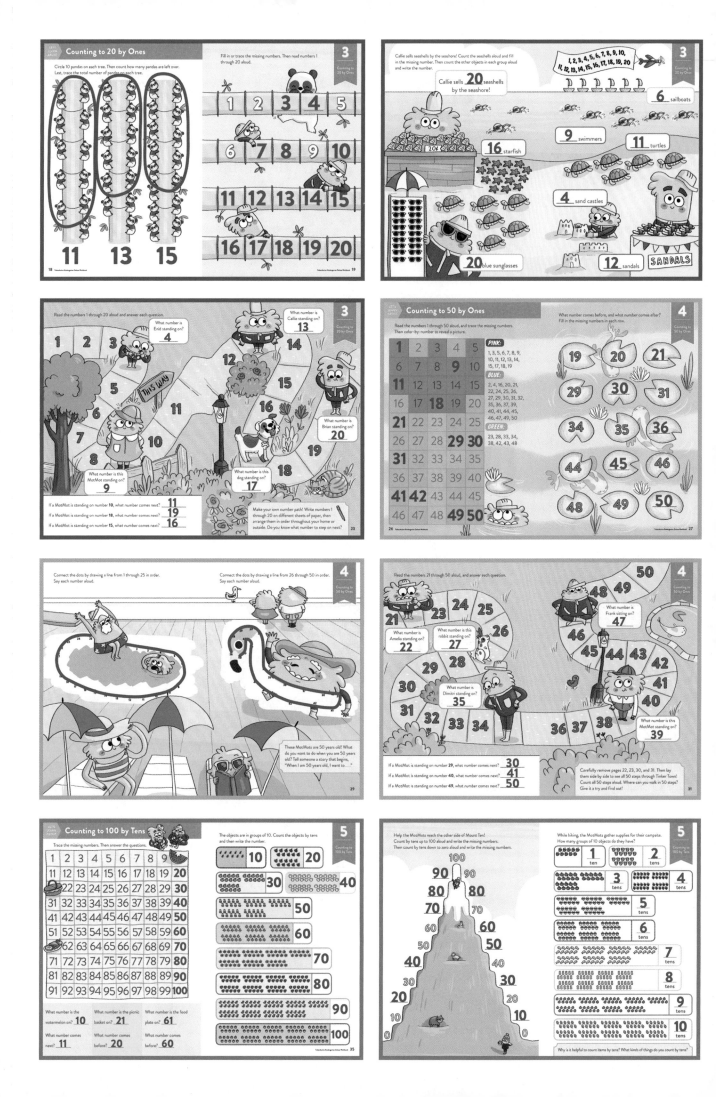

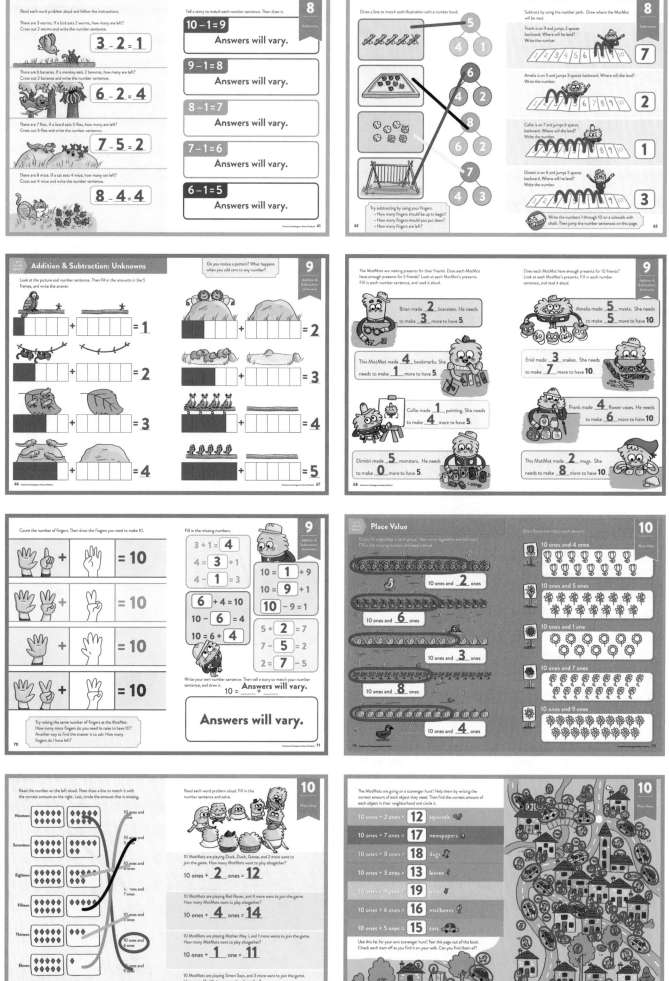

Page 61

Read each word problem aloud and follow the instructions.

There are 3 worms. If a bird eats 2 worms, how many are left? Cross out 2 worms and write the number sentence.
$3 - 2 = 1$

There are 6 bananas. If a monkey eats 2 bananas, how many are left? Cross out 2 bananas and write the number sentence.
$6 - 2 = 4$

There are 7 flies. If a lizard eats 5 flies, how many are left? Cross out 5 flies and write the number sentence.
$7 - 5 = 2$

There are 8 mice. If a cat eats 4 mice, how many are left? Cross out 4 mice and write the number sentence.
$8 - 4 = 4$

Tell a story to match each number sentence. Then draw it.

$10 - 1 = 9$ Answers will vary.

$9 - 1 = 8$ Answers will vary.

$8 - 1 = 7$ Answers will vary.

$7 - 1 = 6$ Answers will vary.

$6 - 1 = 5$ Answers will vary.

Pages 62–63

Draw a line to match each illustration with a number bond.

5 / 4 1
6 / 4 2
8 / 6 2
7 / 4 3

Try subtracting by using your fingers.
- How many fingers should be up to begin?
- How many fingers should you put down?
- How many fingers are left?

Subtract by using the number path. Draw where the MotMot will be next.

Frank is on 9 and jumps 2 spaces backward. Where will he land? Write the number.   7

Amelia is on 5 and jumps 3 spaces backward. Where will she land? Write the number.   2

Callie is on 7 and jumps 6 spaces backward. Where will she land?   1

Dimitri is on 8 and jumps 5 spaces backward. Where will he land? Write the number.   3

Write the numbers 1 through 10 on a sidewalk with chalk. Then jump the number sentences on this page.

Page 66–67

Addition & Subtraction: Unknowns

Look at the picture and number sentence. Then fill in the amounts in the 5 frames, and write the answer.

$\square + \square = 1$
$\square + \square = 2$
$\square + \square = 3$
$\square + \square = 4$

Do you notice a pattern? What happens when you add zero to any number?

$\square + \square = 2$
$\square + \square = 3$
$\square + \square = 4$
$\square + \square = 5$

Page 68–69

The MotMots are making presents for their friends. Does each MotMot have enough presents for 5 friends? Look at each MotMot's presents. Fill in each number sentence, and read it aloud.

Brian made **2** bracelets. He needs to make **3** more to have **5**.

This MotMot made **4** bookmarks. She needs to make **1** more to have **5**.

Callie made **1** painting. She needs to make **4** more to have **5**.

Dimitri made **5** monsters. He needs to make **0** more to have **5**.

Does each MotMot have enough presents for 10 friends? Look at each MotMot's presents. Fill in each number sentence, and read it aloud.

Amelia made **5** masks. She needs to make **5** more to have **10**.

Enid made **3** snakes. She needs to make **7** more to have **10**.

Frank made **4** flower vases. He needs to make **6** more to have **10**.

This MotMot made **2** mugs. She needs to make **8** more to have **10**.

Page 70–71

Count the number of fingers. Then draw the fingers you need to make 10.

$\square + \square = 10$
$\square + \square = 10$
$\square + \square = 10$
$\square + \square = 10$

Try raising the same number of fingers as the MotMot. How many more fingers do you need to raise to have 10? Another way to find the answer is to ask: How many fingers do I have left?

Fill in the missing numbers.

$3 + 1 = \boxed{4}$
$4 = \boxed{3} + 1$
$4 - \boxed{1} = 3$

$10 = \boxed{1} + 9$
$10 = \boxed{9} + 1$
$\boxed{10} - 9 = 1$

$\boxed{6} + 4 = 10$
$10 - \boxed{6} = 4$
$10 = 6 + \boxed{4}$

$5 + \boxed{2} = 7$
$7 - \boxed{5} = 2$
$2 = \boxed{7} - 5$

Write your own number sentence. Then tell a story to match your number sentence, and draw it.

$10 = \underline{\text{Answers will vary.}} + \underline{\quad}$

Answers will vary.

Page 74–75

Place Value

Circle 10 vegetables in each group. How many vegetables are left over? Fill in the missing number, and read it aloud.

10 ones and **2** ones
10 ones and **6** ones
10 ones and **3** ones
10 ones and **8** ones
10 ones and **4** ones

Draw flowers to match each amount.

10 ones and 4 ones
10 ones and 5 ones
10 ones and 1 one
10 ones and 7 ones
10 ones and 9 ones

Page 77

Read the number on the left aloud. Then draw a line to match it with the correct amount on the right. Last, circle the amount that is missing.

Nineteen
Seventeen
Eighteen
Fifteen
Thirteen
Eleven
Twelve

10 ones and 9 ones
10 ones and 5 ones
10 ones and 8 ones
10 ones and 7 ones
10 ones and 6 ones

Read each word problem aloud. Fill in the number sentence and solve.

10 MotMots are playing Duck, Duck, Goose, and 2 more want to join the game. How many MotMots want to play altogether?
10 ones + **2** ones = **12**

10 MotMots are playing Red Rover, and 4 more want to join the game. How many MotMots want to play altogether?
10 ones + **4** ones = **14**

10 MotMots are playing Mother May I, and 1 more wants to join the game. How many MotMots want to play altogether?
10 ones + **1** one = **11**

10 MotMots are playing Simon Says, and 3 more want to join the game. How many MotMots want to play altogether?
10 ones + **3** ones = **13**

Page 79

The MotMots are going on a scavenger hunt! Help them by writing the correct amount of each object they need. Then find the correct amount of each object in their neighborhood and circle it.

10 ones + 2 ones = **12** squirrels
10 ones + 7 ones = **17** newspapers
10 ones + 8 ones = **18** dogs
10 ones + 3 ones = **13** leaves
10 ones + 9 ones = **19** birds
10 ones + 6 ones = **16** mailboxes
10 ones + 5 ones = **15** cars

Use this list for your own scavenger hunt! Tear this page out of the book. Check each item off as you find it on your walk. Can you find them all?

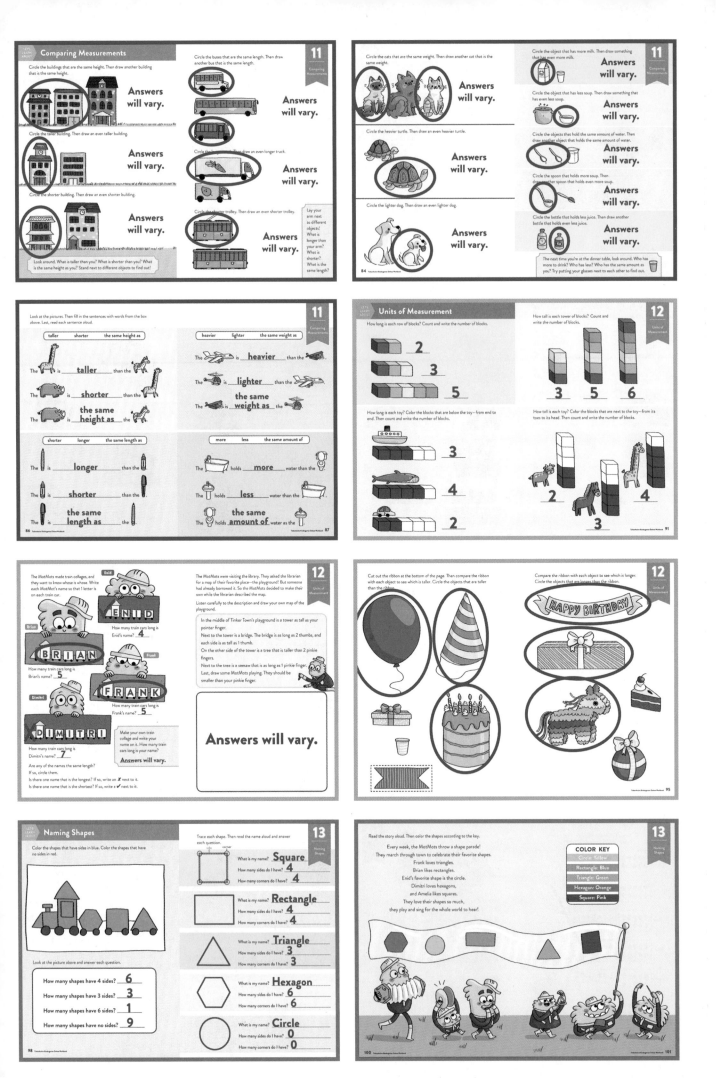

Comparing Measurements

Circle the buildings that are the same height. Then draw another building that is the same height.

Answers will vary.

Circle the taller building. Then draw an even taller building.

Answers will vary.

Circle the shorter building. Then draw an even shorter building.

Answers will vary.

Look around. What is taller than you? What is shorter than you? What is the same height as you? Stand next to different objects to find out!

Circle the buses that are the same length. Then draw another bus that is the same length.

Answers will vary.

Circle the longer truck. Then draw an even longer truck.

Answers will vary.

Circle the shorter trolley. Then draw an even shorter trolley.

Answers will vary.

Lay your arm next to different objects! What is longer than your arm? What is shorter? What is the same length?

Circle the cats that are the same weight. Then draw another cat that is the same weight.

Answers will vary.

Circle the heavier turtle. Then draw an even heavier turtle.

Answers will vary.

Circle the lighter dog. Then draw an even lighter dog.

Answers will vary.

Circle the object that has more milk. Then draw something that has even more milk.

Answers will vary.

Circle the object that has less soup. Then draw something that has even less soup.

Answers will vary.

Circle the objects that hold the same amount of water. Then draw another object that holds the same amount of water.

Answers will vary.

Circle the spoon that holds more soup. Then draw another spoon that holds even more soup.

Answers will vary.

Circle the bottle that holds less juice. Then draw another bottle that holds even less juice.

Answers will vary.

The next time you're at the dinner table, look around. Who has more to drink? Who has less? Who has the same amount as you? Try putting your glasses next to each other to find out.

84

Look at the pictures. Then fill in the sentences with words from the box above. Last, read each sentence aloud.

taller   shorter   the same height as

The 🦒 is **taller** than the 🦓.

The 🦏 is **shorter** than the 🦒.

The 🦏 is **the same height as** the 🦓.

shorter   longer   the same length as

The ✏️ is **longer** than the ✏️.

The ✏️ is **shorter** than the ✏️.

The ✏️ is **the same length as** the ✏️.

heavier   lighter   the same weight as

The ✈️ is **heavier** than the ✈️.

The 🚁 is **lighter** than the ✈️.

The ✈️ is **the same weight as** the 🚁.

more   less   the same amount of

The 🛁 holds **more** water than the 🚽.

The 🚽 holds **less** water than the 🛁.

The 🚽 holds **the same amount of** water as the 🚽.

86

Units of Measurement

How long is each row of blocks? Count and write the number of blocks.

2
3
5

How long is each toy? Color the blocks that are below the toy—from end to end. Then count and write the number of blocks.

3
4
2

How tall is each tower of blocks? Count and write the number of blocks.

3   5   6

How tall is each toy? Color the blocks that are next to the toy—from its toes to its head. Then count and write the number of blocks.

2   4   3

91

The MotMots made train collages, and they want to know whose is whose. Write each MotMot's name so that 1 letter is on each train car.

Enid

ENID

How many train cars long is Enid's name? **4**

Brian

BRIAN

How many train cars long is Brian's name? **5**

Frank

FRANK

How many train cars long is Frank's name? **5**

Dimitri

DIMITRI

How many train cars long is Dimitri's name? **7**

Are any of the names the same length? If so, circle them.
Is there one name that is the longest? If so, write an ✗ next to it.
Is there one name that is the shortest? If so, write a ✔ next to it.

Make your own train collage and write your name on it. How many train cars long is your name?

Answers will vary.

The MotMots were visiting the library. They asked the librarian for a map of their favorite place—the playground! But someone had already borrowed it. So the MotMots decided to make their own while the librarian described the map.

Listen carefully to the description and draw your own map of the playground.

In the middle of Tinker Town's playground is a tower as tall as your pointer finger.
Next to the tower is a bridge. The bridge is as long as 2 thumbs, and each side is as tall as 1 thumb.
On the other side of the tower is a tree that is taller than 2 pinkie fingers.
Next to the tree is a seesaw that is as long as 1 pinkie finger.
Last, draw some MotMots playing. They should be smaller than your pinkie finger.

Answers will vary.

Cut out the ribbon at the bottom of the page. Then compare the ribbon with each object to see which is taller. Circle the objects that are taller than the ribbon.

Compare the ribbon with each object to see which is longer. Circle the objects that are longer than the ribbon.

HAPPY BIRTHDAY

95

Naming Shapes

Color the shapes that have sides in blue. Color the shapes that have no sides in red.

Look at the picture above and answer each question.

How many shapes have 4 sides?	**6**
How many shapes have 3 sides?	**3**
How many shapes have 6 sides?	**1**
How many shapes have no sides?	**9**

Trace each shape. Then read the name aloud and answer each question.

What is my name? **Square**
How many sides do I have? **4**
How many corners do I have? **4**

What is my name? **Rectangle**
How many sides do I have? **4**
How many corners do I have? **4**

What is my name? **Triangle**
How many sides do I have? **3**
How many corners do I have? **3**

What is my name? **Hexagon**
How many sides do I have? **6**
How many corners do I have? **6**

What is my name? **Circle**
How many sides do I have? **0**
How many corners do I have? **0**

98

Read the story aloud. Then color the shapes according to the key.

Every week, the MotMots throw a shape parade!
They march through town to celebrate their favorite shapes.
Frank loves triangles.
Brian likes rectangles.
Enid's favorite shape is the circle.
Dimitri loves hexagons,
and Amelia likes squares.
They love their shapes so much,
they play and sing for the whole world to hear!

COLOR KEY
Circle: Yellow
Rectangle: Blue
Triangle: Green
Hexagon: Orange
Square: Pink

100   101

If you put shapes together, you can make something new!
Draw a line to match the groups of shapes with the new shape.

With an adult's help, cut out the shapes on the previous page and use the pieces to make each shape below. Then fill in each sentence.

I made a triangle out of
2 triangles

I made a square out of
2 rectangles

I made a square out of
2 triangles

I made a rectangle out of
2 squares

I made a hexagon out of
6 triangles

The only shape I didn't use was a **circle**

Spatial Reasoning

The MotMots are on safari! Tell them where each animal is by tracing the words and reading each sentence aloud.

A bird is **above** the tree.

The zebras are **behind** the trees.

The lions are **beside** the watering hole.

The lion cub is **in** its mother's mouth.

The giraffe is **next to** the watering hole.

A bird is **on** the hippo.

The baby elephant is **below** his mother.

The snake is **beside** the rocks.

The warthogs are **in front of** the bush.

The meerkat is **next to** the bush.

The mouse is **in front of** the anthill.

The deer is **behind** the anthill.

Circle the word that completes each sentence. Then read the sentence aloud.

Callie is
beside below
the umbrella

Brian is
next to on
a worm.

Amelia is
in front of behind
a frog.

Dimitri is
in front of below
the flowers.

Frank is
below **on**
the rock.

Frank is
in above
the puddle.

Enid made a rainy-day collage! Look at the collage and complete each sentence.

| circle | rectangle | hexagon | triangle |

I have **3 sides**, and I am above Enid. I am a **triangle**

I have **4 sides**, and I am in front of the trees. I am a **rectangle**

I have **no sides**, and I am behind the clouds. I am a **circle**

I have **6 sides**, and I am next to the bench. I am a **hexagon**

Create a model of space! With an adult's help, cut out the objects below and paste them on the following page according to the directions.

Paste the Sun beside Mercury.

Paste Neptune next to Uranus.

Paste Saturn's ring on Saturn.

Paste the space shuttle and astronaut wherever you like.

Paste the stars above and below the planets.

Mercury
Venus
Earth
Mars
Jupiter
Saturn
Uranus

Fill in the sentences:

I pasted the space shuttle _____
Answers will vary.

I pasted the astronaut _____
Answers will vary.

Shapes

Is each shape 2-dimensional or 3-dimensional? Color the flat, 2-dimensional shapes in red. Color the solid, 3-dimensional shapes in blue.

Circle the object that has the same face or surface as the 2-dimensional shape.

Trace each shape. Then read the name aloud, and answer each question.

What is my name? **Cube**
How many faces do I have? **6**
How many corners do I have? **8**

What is my name? **Rectangular Prism**
How many faces do I have? **6**
How many corners do I have? **8**

What is my name? **Pyramid**
How many faces do I have? **5**
How many corners do I have? **5**

What is my name? **Cylinder**
How many faces do I have? **2**
How many corners do I have? **0**

What is my name? **Sphere**
How many faces do I have? **0**
How many corners do I have? **0**

Match each name to its shape by drawing a line through the maze. If you pass a sign, read it aloud for a hint.

Answers will vary.

cube
rectangular prism
cylinder
cone
pyramid
sphere

I have 6 square faces.
I have 2 circle faces.
I have 5 corners.
I have no faces.

Go on a shape scavenger hunt! Look at each shape and trace the name. Then find objects in your home that are or have the same shapes. Draw each object below.

rectangular prism
Answers will vary.

cube
Answers will vary.

cylinder
Answers will vary.

sphere
Answers will vary.

pyramid
Answers will vary.

cone
Answers will vary.

TinkerActive WORKBOOKS

KINDERGARTEN · SCIENCE · AGES 5–6

by Megan Hewes Butler

illustrated by Taryn Johnson

educational consulting by Randi House

 Odd Dot · New York

Weather

The weather is made up of many things: sunlight, wind, temperature, and even snow or rain. The weather is always changing.

Draw the weather you remember from yesterday.

Write a ✔ to mark the weather that happened yesterday.

☐ sunshine ☐ clouds ☐ wind ☐ rain ☐ snow

Observe and draw the weather today.

Write a ✔ to mark the weather that happened today.

☐ sunshine ☐ clouds ☐ wind ☐ rain ☐ snow

Look at each picture and say your own weather report aloud. Then fill in the words that describe the weather in each picture.

sunny and warm   cloudy   windy and cold

Report: _____

Report: _____

Report: _____

Draw your own weather forecast for tomorrow.

Circle the items you would wear for each kind of weather.

SNOWSTORM

HEAT WAVE

COLD AND WINDY

Imagine that you are going from your home to the school bus in each of these weather conditions. Act out what you would do.

• Would you run? • Splash? • Hold on to your hat?

LET'S START! GATHER THESE TOOLS AND MATERIALS.

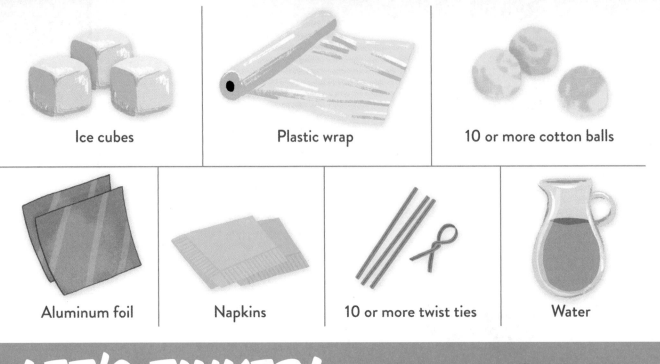

Ice cubes

Plastic wrap

10 or more cotton balls

Aluminum foil

Napkins

10 or more twist ties

Water

LET'S TINKER!

Get an ice cube.

Rub the ice cube on the other materials.

What happens when the ice touches the other materials? How does each material change? Does it become warmer or colder? Does it stay dry or become wet?

LET'S MAKE: MINI WEATHER!

1. **Draw** each weather event.

2. **Use** your materials to make models of the weather based on your drawings.

Clouds

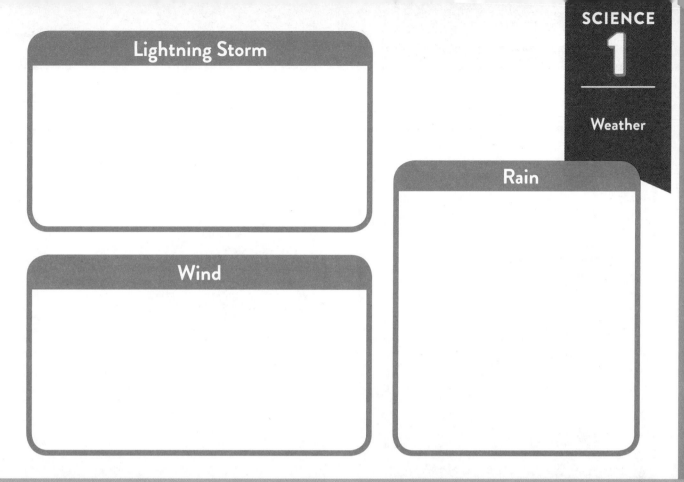

Lightning Storm

Wind

Rain

LET'S ENGINEER!

Meet Fluffy, Frank's pet cotton ball. Frank likes to play with Fluffy outdoors, and they both need to stay warm and dry.

How can Frank protect Fluffy from the weather?

Make a protective layer to keep Fluffy warm and dry. Which materials work best to protect her? How can the materials be combined to help?

Test your design with water and an ice cube. Does the cotton ball stay warm and dry?

PROJECT 1: DONE!
Get your sticker!

Trace the name of each season.

Summer

Fall

Winter

Spring

The changing weather each season brings new activities.
Circle the gear Callie can use in each season.

SUMMER

FALL

WINTER

SPRING

A pattern is something that repeats. Our planet has patterns.
Day and night repeat every day, and the four seasons repeat every year.

Look at each pattern. Then fill in the missing word.

Day   Night   Day   Night   _____

Sunrise   Sunset   Sunrise   Sunset   _____

Summer   Fall   Winter   Spring   Summer   _____

Winter   _____   Summer   Fall   _____   Spring

Write about and draw pictures of the patterns you see near you.

Look out your window. Circle which season it is now.

Draw what you see that tells you what season it is.

Circle the activities that you can do during this season.

LET'S START!

GATHER THESE TOOLS AND MATERIALS.

Crayons	10 or more cotton balls	10 or more twist ties	Measuring cup
Baking soda	Hair conditioner	Bowl	Spoon	Paper

LET'S TINKER!

The seasons are one of Earth's patterns.

Make your own patterns with your materials. Which materials can repeat? Which materials can be combined? Can you make short patterns? Long ones?

LET'S MAKE: INDOOR SNOW!

1. With an adult's help, **mix** 3 cups of baking soda and $\frac{1}{2}$ cup of hair conditioner in a bowl.

2. Place the bowl in your freezer for a few hours to make it feel cold, or just play with your indoor snow right away.

What does the snow feel like in your hands? What does it sound like when you move it around? Can you make a snowball?

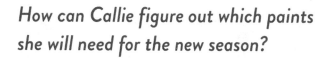

LET'S ENGINEER!

Callie loves to paint the tree outside her bedroom window. It's summer, and she only needs brown and green paints. But the season is about to change.

How can Callie figure out which paints she will need for the new season?

Record what season it is now and predict what will happen to the tree in the next season.

Draw a picture of a tree near you now. Then **draw** how it will look in the other three seasons. What colors do you need? What happens to the leaves? What other changes do you see?

PROJECT 2: DONE!
Get your sticker!

Severe Weather

Some types of severe weather are a tornado, a hurricane, and a blizzard.
Describe each picture. Then, trace the name of the weather event.

cloud

funnel

Tornado

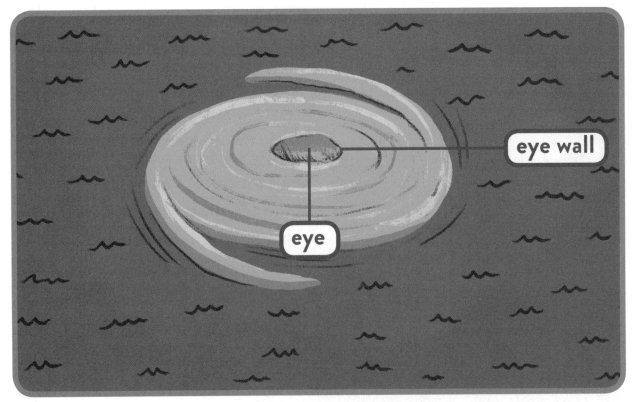

eye wall

eye

Hurricane

cloud

wind

snow

Blizzard

Other types of severe weather include a flood, a heat wave, and fog.
Draw a picture of a type of severe weather you've seen.

Read aloud about each type of severe weather. Then draw lines
from each storm to the ways you can prepare to stay safe.
(Hint: there may be more than one correct answer.)

TORNADO

A tornado forms when high-speed wind stretches from a cloud down to the ground. The wind forms a spinning column of air called a funnel.

HURRICANE

A hurricane is a big storm that starts over the ocean. Winds whirl the storm around very quickly, bringing bands of heavy rain.

Shelter in a safe place.

Board up windows.

Write about or draw what you would do to stay safe in severe weather.

BLIZZARD

A blizzard is a strong snowstorm with high winds. The winds blow very fast—faster than a horse can run!

A storm chaser is someone who heads toward severe weather instead of away from it!

Some scientists and news reporters must get close to storms to do their jobs. You should go to a safe place, however.

Gather supplies.

Stay inside a warm place.

Write about or draw a safe place in your home.

Draw a line through the maze to help Callie gather all the emergency supplies and then take them to her home.

First aid kit

Food

How can these
items help you in
a severe storm?

_____

_____

_____

_____

_____

Water

Flashlight and
batteries

Emergency
radio

LET'S START!

GATHER THESE TOOLS AND MATERIALS.

Large bowl	Water	10 or more paper clips	10 or more pennies
Drinking straw	10 or more cotton balls	Aluminum foil	Paper	Crayons

LET'S TINKER!

Fill a bowl with water and drop a paper clip into the water.

Next **try** dropping in a penny, a straw, a cotton ball, and a piece of foil. Do they sink or float? Do they move quickly or slowly? How do they change?

LET'S MAKE: TINY TORNADO!

1. **Make** tiny tornado art with your materials.

2. **Show** the funnel of high wind. Which materials look like a cloud that a tornado could come from? What happens when the tornado reaches the ground in your art?

Amelia loves spinning around like a hurricane. She wants to know if she spins faster with her arms out or tucked in.

How can Amelia observe how fast an object spins?

Stir water in a bowl to make the water spin like a hurricane.

Drop a paper clip into the water and make it move as fast as you can.

Does the paper clip move faster when it's in the middle of the bowl? Or does it move faster along the edge of the bowl?

Can you drop the paper clip into the eye—the exact center of the bowl of water? How will you know if you got it in the eye?

How do the other materials act when you drop them into the spinning water?

Water

All living things need water. This includes plants, animals, and people, too! Circle the things on these two pages that are living.

Draw a line to connect each living thing to a place where it usually gets water.

Read the poem aloud.

Then draw a line to help Callie take her hose to water all of the flowers.

Callie, Callie, in the valley, how does your garden grow? By dragging the hose through all of the rows, to where the water should flow.

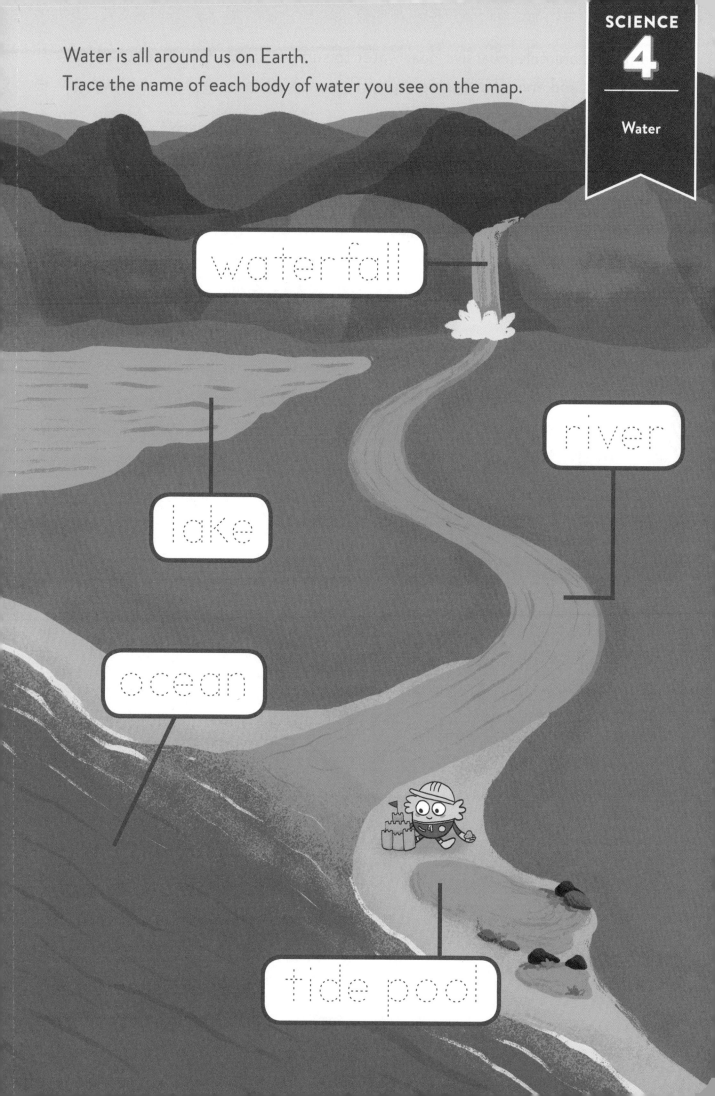

Water is all around us on Earth.
Trace the name of each body of water you see on the map.

waterfall

river

lake

ocean

tide pool

Plants and animals must live near water to survive. Circle the water used by each plant and animal in each picture. Then name the water source aloud.

 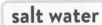

rain   salt water   lake   stream

Go on a scavenger hunt around your home. Draw pictures of the places where you get the water you need.

Water for drinking

Water for keeping clean

Water for cooking

Sandwich bag	Toilet paper roll	Aluminum foil	Paper
Rubber bands	Crayons	6 or more coins	4–6 paper clips

LET'S TINKER!

Think about which of your materials can help living things get the water they need. Can a pet drink from any of these objects? Can any of the objects carry water to a plant? Can you use any of them to drink from? Which ones won't hold any water?

Try using your materials to bring water to a plant or pet.

LET'S MAKE: WATERY WEATHER!

1. **Make** models of different types of watery weather.

2. **Draw** raindrops, arrange your materials like a snowflake, or even tear, roll, and squish the foil into hail.

   Can you use the other materials to make watery weather models?

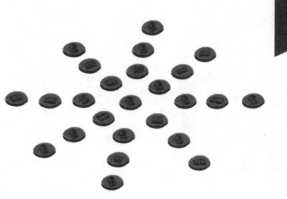

LET'S ENGINEER!

Enid just planted a beautiful flower. She wants to know if it is getting enough water.

How can Enid study the amount of rain that falls on her flower?

Create a tool that will capture and hold some of the rain that falls.

Test your design in a sink. Does the water stay inside the tool? Can you see how much water has fallen into your tool?

What might happen if instead of water from the faucet, your tool caught snow, rain, or hail?

Place your tool outside.

Draw a picture of your tool after it rains or snows.

Add to your picture every time it rains or snows.

PROJECT 4: DONE!
Get your sticker!

The Sun

Look at Earth. When one side is facing the Sun, it's daytime there. That's when the air is warmed by the Sun. On the other side, away from the Sun, it's nighttime there. That's when it's cooler. Circle the warm side with red. Circle the cool side with blue.

The Sun rises and sets at different times in different places throughout the year.

Around what time did the Sun rise near you this morning?
Were you awake?

Watch to see what time it sets tonight—if you are awake to see it!

Look what the Sun is melting! Draw what happens to each item in the hot Sun.

The Sun warms Earth. How do you stay cool when it's hot outside?

Read the story aloud.

Amelia, Brian, Callie, and Dimitri are at the playground. It's a sunny day. Amelia enjoys taking a picnic lunch. Yum! Brian heads straight for the monkey bars. He likes to climb and swing. Wheeeee! Callie jumps into her favorite place to dig. Scoop! Dimitri wants to go down the slide, but it is too hot. Ouch!

Brian

Amelia

Help the MotMots cool off:

- Draw an umbrella to shade Amelia's picnic.

- Draw a hat to cover Brian on the monkey bars.

- Draw a giant tent over the sandbox for Callie.

- Draw a tree to shade the slide for Dimitri.

Callie

Dimitri

When the Sun hits an object, the object makes a shadow on the ground. Where the Sun no longer reaches the ground, it's cooler. Draw the missing shadows.

Go outside into the Sun and make your own shadow on the ground. Draw your shadow here.

It's a blazing hot day, and Dimitri needs to buy a hat!
Draw a line on the sidewalk to take him to the hat
shop while staying in the shade.

HATS

LET'S START!

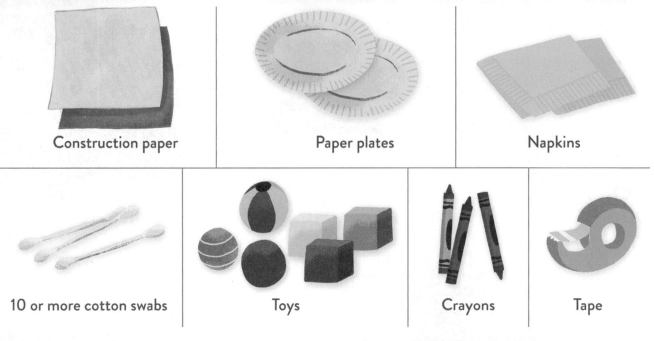

Construction paper

Paper plates

Napkins

10 or more cotton swabs

Toys

Crayons

Tape

LET'S TINKER!

Use sunlight or a light to make shadows with your body and your materials. What happens when you move closer to a light? What about farther away from it? Can you make shadows on the floor or on the wall?

LET'S MAKE: SHADOW ART!

1. Lay a piece of paper flat.

2. Make a shadow on the paper with your body or with another object.

3. Trace the shadow with crayons and color it in to make shadow art.

You can also make a reverse shadow!

1. **Place** a sheet of dark construction paper outside, in the bright sun.

2. **Lay** an object (like a toy or a cotton swab) on the paper.

3. After a few hours, **pick** up the object. What do you see on the paper?

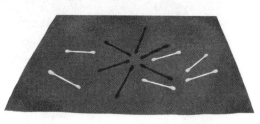

LET'S ENGINEER!

Brian is throwing the world's smallest ice-cream party for his good friends the ants, but the weather is predicted to be sunny and hot.

How can Brian keep the ice cream cool so it doesn't melt as fast?

Make a structure that can shade ice cream. Which materials can help block the Sun? Which materials can hold the structure in place?

World's Smallest Ice-Cream Party!

PROJECT 5: DONE!
Get your sticker!

Parts of a Plant

Plants have many parts to help them live and grow.

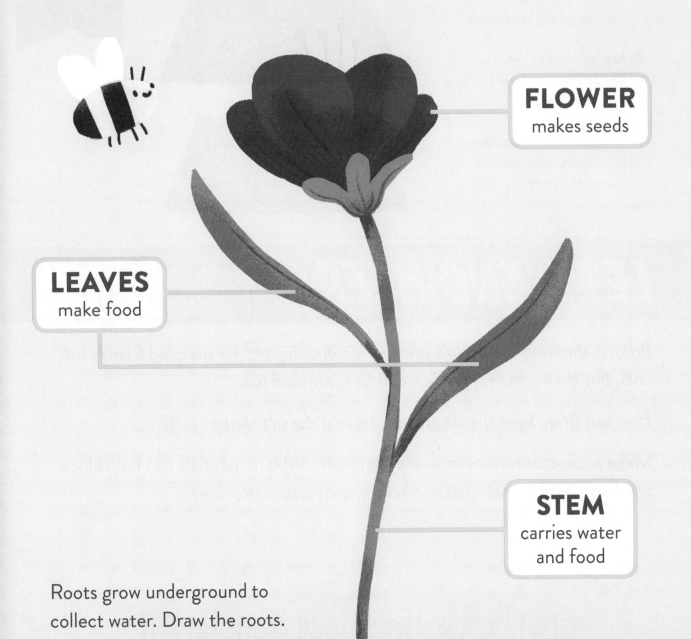

FLOWER
makes seeds

LEAVES
make food

STEM
carries water
and food

Roots grow underground to
collect water. Draw the roots.

Leaves collect sunlight to make food for the plant.
Draw the leaves.

BRANCHES
carry water and food

TRUNK
supports the
tree

ROOTS
collect water

Go outside and look around your home. Which parts
of flowers, trees, and other plants can you see?

Read Enid's poem aloud.

I Like Plants, Yes I Do

I eat plants, that's what I like.

When I'm hungry, I take a hike.

Tubers, bulbs, and flowers, too.

Roots and seeds are what I chew.

Did you know you can eat a stem?

Celery, asparagus—I pick them!

Leaves seem to be what I like best.

But I couldn't live without the rest.

Plants are tasty—want to see?

Just come and take a hike with me!

LEAVES

SEEDS

FLOWERS

ROOTS

Draw the parts of plants that you like to eat below.

Many plants spread seeds to grow new plants. Seeds come in many different shapes, sizes, and colors, but inside they have the same parts:

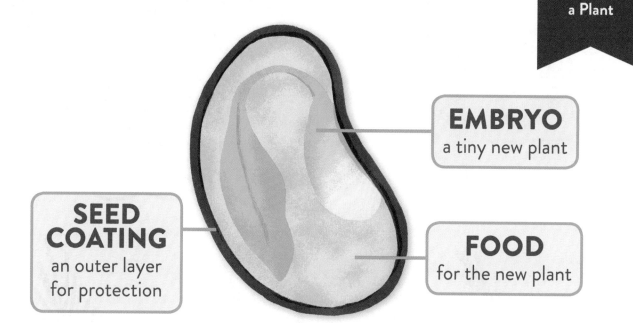

EMBRYO
a tiny new plant

SEED COATING
an outer layer for protection

FOOD
for the new plant

Circle the seeds in each fruit and vegetable.

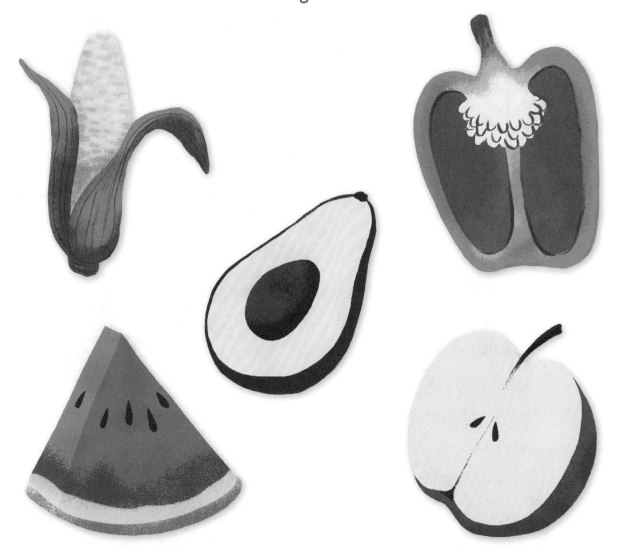

Different types of plants have different leaves:

lily pads

fern fronds

grass-blades

pine needles

cactus spines

clover leaves

Observe a plant.
Draw the parts you can see.

Find a plant. Draw the parts that you can't see, under the dirt.

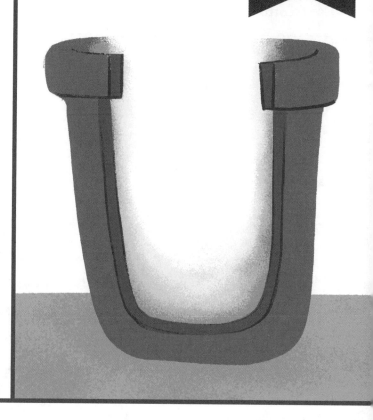

Pick a leaf from a tree or plant. Then trace it here.

LET'S START! GATHER THESE TOOLS AND MATERIALS.

4–6 cotton balls	4–6 twist ties	4–6 rubber bands	4–6 drinking straws
Toilet paper roll	Large cup	Water	Celery stalk with leaves or a white flower	Food coloring

LET'S TINKER!

Use your materials to show the different parts of a plant.

Try making a model that lies flat on a table or stands upright.

Include roots, a stem or trunk, and leaves.

LET'S MAKE: STEM EXPERIMENT!

A stem carries water and food up and down a plant. **Watch** a stem at work!

1. Place a stalk of celery or a white flower in a cup of water. You may need to break or cut off a small piece of the stem first.

2. Add several drops of food coloring to the water.

3. Predict what the stem will do with the colored water. Do you notice any changes right away?

4. Check back the next day. What changes do you see? What work does the stem do? What do you think will happen if you leave the stem in the water?

LET'S ENGINEER!

Callie wants to teach Dimitri how seeds grow in many different shapes and sizes—but she doesn't have any seeds!

How can Callie teach Dimitri without seeds?

Design a model of your own seed.

How can you use one of your materials to represent the tough outer shell of a seed? What can you make to represent the food inside? Which materials can hold everything together? How does your seed travel—can it float or fly?

PROJECT 6: DONE!
Get your sticker!

Plant Survival

Plants need sunlight, water, air, and nutrients from the dirt to grow.

Help this plant grow. Draw a window for sunlight and air, dirt for nutrients, and a watering can to water it with.

Circle each plant that has the sunlight, water, air, and nutrients from dirt that it needs. For the plants that you did not circle, fill in what each plant needs.

| sunlight | water | dirt |

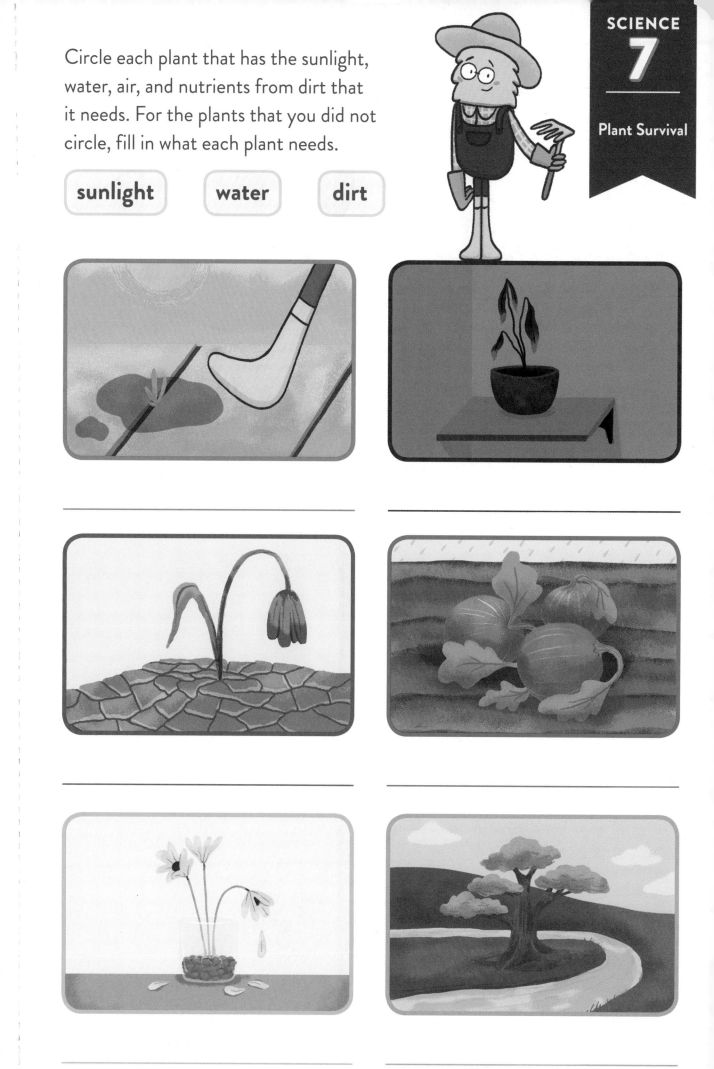

The MotMots have each planted different seeds. First, say aloud how they can take care of their seeds. Then draw a picture of what you think will grow from the seeds.

PUMPKIN SEEDS

GRASS SEEDS

APPLE SEEDS

SUNFLOWER SEEDS

There are many different kinds of plants, but they all need the same things to grow: sunlight, water, air, and nutrients from the dirt. Cross out the things that each plant does not need to survive.

Imagine that you have your own plant. Look around your home:
- What would you plant it in?
- What would you use to give it water?
- Where could you put it so it had sunlight and air?

Draw a picture of your plant. Also draw yourself taking care of it.

LET'S START! GATHER THESE TOOLS AND MATERIALS.

Water	Washcloth	Sponge	Paper	Rubber bands
Small cup	3–5 paper towels	Sandwich bag		3–5 dried beans (lima beans, white beans, or black beans)

LET'S TINKER!

Wet some of your materials, first just a little, and then a lot.

Watch what happens when these materials get a little wet.

See what happens when they get very wet. Can you make them dry again? Can you move water from one material to another?

LET'S MAKE: GROW A SEED!

Plants need sunlight, water, air, and nutrients to grow. **Make** an environment to grow your own bean seedling!

1. Fold a wet paper towel and place it inside a sandwich bag.

2. Place a few dried beans on top of the paper towel and seal the bag shut.

3. **Place** the bag by a window. What do you think the bean seeds will do? How long do you think it will take to see a change in them?

4. **Watch** the bean seeds for several days. What plant parts do you see?

LET'S ENGINEER!

It hasn't rained in Tinker Town in many days, and Dimitri has very little water for his plants. All of his plants look like they need more water—except for his cactus.

How can Dimitri store water like a cactus?

Use the materials together to hold as much water as possible.

PROJECT 7: DONE!
Get your sticker!

Animal Survival

We can study and sort animals by what they eat to survive.

CARNIVORE: an animal that only eats other animals

OMNIVORE: an animal that eats both animals and plants

HERBIVORE: an animal that only eats plants

Do you eat animals, plants, or both? Write your name under **carnivore**, **omnivore**, or **herbivore** above. Then draw what you eat in the box to the right.

Observe what each animal eats. Then write each animal's name next to **carnivore**, **omnivore**, or **herbivore**.

PENGUINS

ZEBRA

BEARS

CARNIVORE: _____

OMNIVORE: _____

HERBIVORE: _____

All animals need to eat food and drink water to live and grow. But different animals eat different foods. Draw a line to connect each animal to what it likes to eat.

**A goat is an
HERBIVORE.**

It eats only plants.

**A squirrel is an
OMNIVORE.**

It eats plants
and animals.

**A lion is a
CARNIVORE.**

It eats only
animals.

Read the text aloud. Look closely at the pictures on the next page.
Fill in the blanks with the name of the correct animal.

Squirrel It Away

Some animals store food to eat later. A _____

likes to eat seeds and nuts. It can carry them tucked into its

large cheeks and bury extras underground in its burrow. Then

when it hibernates in the winter, it has food to eat when it

wakes up briefly every few days.

Another animal that stores food is a _____.

It eats leaves, bark, and roots. It carries food underwater

to its home, called a lodge, where it lives during the cold

winter months.

A _____ also stores food underground, because

it spends most of its life there. This

animal makes many underground

tunnels, including an

underground kitchen to

store worms in. Some tunnel

kitchens have been found

with hundreds of

worms inside!

MOLE

BEAVER

CHIPMUNK

LET'S START!

GATHER THESE TOOLS AND MATERIALS.

Pencil

10 or more rubber bands or shredded newspaper

Waxed paper

Books

Piece of string 3–5 feet long

Tape

Paper

4–6 plastic cups

LET'S TINKER!

Some animals use camouflage to hide from other animals that want to eat them. *Camouflage* makes them hard to see because they blend in and look like the things around them.

Camouflage a pencil in a pile of rubber bands or shredded newspaper.

Which other materials can you use to cover the pencil to help it blend in?

LET'S MAKE: PRESSED LEAVES!

Herbivores eat leaves and flowers. **Study** and save some leaves and flowers from around your home!

1. **Collect** some leaves and small flowers. (Larger flowers or flowers that are thick and round will not work well.)

2. Tear off a sheet of waxed paper and fold it in half.

3. Lay the leaves and flowers flat inside the folded sheet of waxed paper, making sure the paper covers the bottom and top of each leaf and flower.

4. Place the piece of waxed paper under a stack of heavy books to press the plants flat.

5. Check back in 1 to 2 weeks to see if the leaves and flowers are dried and flat. What other changes happened to the leaves and flowers? What color are the leaves and flowers that you pressed?

LET'S ENGINEER!

Enid wants to make a bug pie for her spider friends. Spiders get food by spinning webs to trap insects. But Enid can't spin a web.

How can Enid trap some bugs for the pie?

Make an insect trap using your materials. How will insects get inside the trap? Will they crawl or fly inside? Can your trap be used indoors or outdoors? Will your trap work on the ground, on a chair, or on the wall?

PROJECT 8: DONE!
Get your sticker!

Animal Habitats

Animals live close to the things they need to survive, like food, water, and shelter. This place is called their habitat. Draw a line to connect each animal to its habitat. Then trace the name of each habitat.

grassland

ocean

rain forest

desert

Anteaters eat more than 35,000 ants a day! They live in forests and grasslands, where there are many anthills.

Draw a line through the maze to connect the anteater to all the anthills. Avoid the hungry pumas—they want to eat the anteater!

Bald eagles eat small birds and mammals, but they mainly eat fish! They live in forests near oceans, rivers, or lakes, where they can find food.

Draw a line through the maze to connect the bald eagle to all the fish. Avoid the bobcats—they want to eat the eagle!

Observe the bees in their habitat. Label the **food**, **water**, and **shelter** that they use.

Walk around in your habitat at home. Then draw a picture of yourself in your habitat. Label the food, water, and shelter that you use.

LET'S START!

GATHER THESE TOOLS AND MATERIALS.

Stick | Paper bag | Dirt | Leaves | Rocks

Shoebox | Grass or a shredded newspaper | Water | Cardboard box

LET'S TINKER!

Many types of animals live right outside your front door. The area around your home is their habitat.

Choose a safe place to sit and explore the ground near your home.

Investigate by looking closely. What materials do you see on the dirt? Are there blades of grass, leaves, or seeds? Sand? Moss? Any insects? Are there any materials you can't identify?

Use a stick to dig a little hole in the dirt. How does the dirt change as you go beneath the surface? What new materials do you see?

Take a paper bag with you, and save some of the materials you've found for the next activities.

LET'S MAKE: LOCAL HABITAT!

What insects and animals do you see outside your home?

1. **Make** a diorama—a model of a habitat—for your favorite local animal.

2. **Use** a shoebox and some of the materials you collected. **Include** materials that represent the food, water, and shelter that this animal needs. Does the animal need anything else to survive?

LET'S ENGINEER!

There's a rabbit in Amelia's backyard. But winter is coming!

How can Amelia keep the rabbit warm?

Make a model shelter for Amelia's new friend.

Use a cardboard box and some of the materials that you found outside in your habitat, like sticks, leaves, and rocks. Which materials are strong enough to shelter a rabbit? What kind of door or opening can you build so a rabbit can go in and out?

PROJECT 9: DONE!
Get your sticker!

Animals & the Environment

Animals change the environments that they live in. Follow the footprints of each animal and trace the path. Then circle what each animal has changed in the forest.

Read aloud about how beavers make their homes.

Timber!

First beavers use their strong

teeth to chop down a tree.

Next they drag the tree branches

to a river. There they can

easily move the branches

in the water.

Then they stack

the branches

and add stones,

leaves, and mud

to create a dam. The dam floods the nearby ground and makes a

pond where plants and animals like fish, ducks, and frogs can live.

Last the beavers build an island called a lodge in the middle of

the new pond. They live

inside the lodge, safe

from predators, like

wolves and bears.

When animals change the environments they live in, sometimes the changes help plants and other animals. But sometimes the changes harm plants and other animals.

Draw some animals that could be helped by the pond that the beaver made.

Color a plant and an animal that were harmed by the beaver's changes.

Circle the pictures that show changes animals have made to the environment. Cross out the pictures that show changes a person has made.

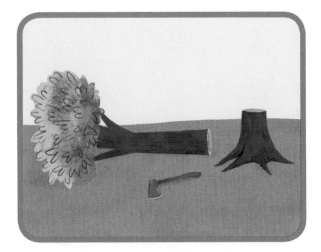

Draw a clue you've seen outside that tells you animals are nearby.

LET'S START!

GATHER THESE TOOLS AND MATERIALS.

Mud or modeling clay	4–6 sticks	4–6 leaves	4–6 rocks	Paper
Ink pad or finger paint	Markers	Plate	Water	

LET'S TINKER!

Press some of your materials into the clay or mud. What happens when the different materials touch the clay? Does the clay change when you press the material on it firmly or softly?

Make your own imprint by pressing your finger or hand into the clay. **Try** a fingerprint, thumbprint, handprint—even an elbow print! How does the clay change?

LET'S MAKE: FINGERPRINT ART!

1. **Press** your fingers on an ink pad or into some finger paint.

2. **Make** fingerprints on a piece of paper.

3. Try making some fingerprints close together and some far apart. What happens when you print them on top of one another?

4. Make some small fingerprints with your pinkie finger and some large ones with your thumb.

5. Use markers to add eyes, legs, wheels, and more to your fingerprints! Can you make a picture of yourself? Or a picture of one of the MotMots? You can also add stickers from page 387.

LET'S ENGINEER!

Frank found a large anthill that he wants to study. The ants are all so busy! However, the anthill is right next to a river, and more rain has been forecasted for later today. What if the river floods?

How can Frank protect the anthill from the river?

Get a plate and add some water to act as a river.

Then **use** your materials to design your own dam. Which materials can help keep the water on one side of the plate?

Test your solution.

PROJECT 10: DONE!
Get your sticker!

People & the Environment

People use resources found in the environment. These are called **natural resources**. Some examples are sunlight, water, plants, animals, and minerals from the ground.

Draw a line from the box to each of the natural resources.

NATURAL RESOURCES

Draw a line to connect each natural resource to a way people use it.

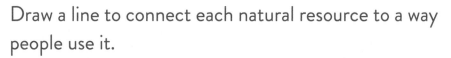

Trees are a natural resource that are used to make paper.
Read the poem aloud.

Paper, Please!

Paper, paper, made from trees.

How's it made? Show me, please!

Trees are cut, the rough bark ripped.

The inside wood is chopped and chipped.

Steam and chemicals do their job.

The fibers make a pulpy glob.

The pulp is dried and spread out thin,

then slid right between some rolling pins.

Cut it up, and stack it high—

the paper's ready for you and I!

Write the numbers 1, 2, 3, and 4 to put the pictures showing how to make paper in order.

Draw a line to show which natural resource each object is made from. Then circle the things you use.

paper

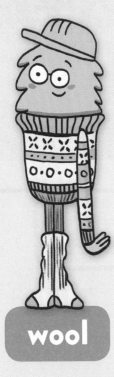

wool

glass

plant

mineral

animal

Look around your home. Draw something else that you use.
Write whether it is made from an animal, a mineral, or a plant.

I use _____.

It is made from _____.

LET'S START!

GATHER THESE TOOLS AND MATERIALS.

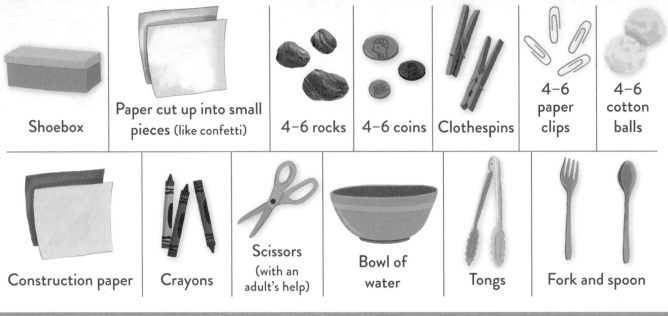

Shoebox	Paper cut up into small pieces (like confetti)	4–6 rocks	4–6 coins	Clothespins	4–6 paper clips	4–6 cotton balls
Construction paper	Crayons	Scissors (with an adult's help)	Bowl of water	Tongs	Fork and spoon	

LET'S TINKER!

Mix together all the materials except the scissors, bowl of water, tongs, fork, and spoon inside the shoebox. Do they stay separate materials or blend together? What happens to the heavy materials?

Sort the natural resources from the man-made materials. Which of the man-made materials are made from natural resources?

LET'S MAKE: PAPER FLOWERS!

Paper is made from a natural resource—trees!—and contains plant fibers. **Make** a paper flower to see how the plant fibers soak up water.

1. Draw a circle in the middle of a small piece of paper and add petals around it.

2. Cut around the outside of the petals.

3. **Fold** the petals all the way up into the middle of the circle.

4. **Place** your flower in the bowl of water.

5. **Watch** how the flower changes in the water. **Check** again in 1 minute, and then several minutes later. Do you see any more changes?

LET'S ENGINEER!

A windstorm blew through Tinker Town on garbage day, and now there is litter everywhere.

How can Enid remove the bits of trash easily?

Use your shoebox full of materials as a model.

The confetti represents trash and the other materials are items that belong in the town, like plants, animals, buildings, and MotMots.

How can you remove the confetti? Why is it difficult to separate? Are there any tools that would make it easier?

PROJECT 11: DONE!
Get your sticker!

Reduce, Reuse, Recycle

We can reduce, reuse, and recycle to help Earth.

Reducing means making less trash and wasting fewer resources with the choices we make every day. Circle the MotMots that are saving Earth by reducing trash and waste.

Write about or draw one way that you can reduce trash in your home or school.

Reusing means using things again instead of throwing them away.

Read Amelia's poem. Then draw a way to reuse each of the things pictured.

Throw it away?
No way!
Toss it in the trash?
News flash—
you can use it again
now and then,
and that's why you choose
to reuse!

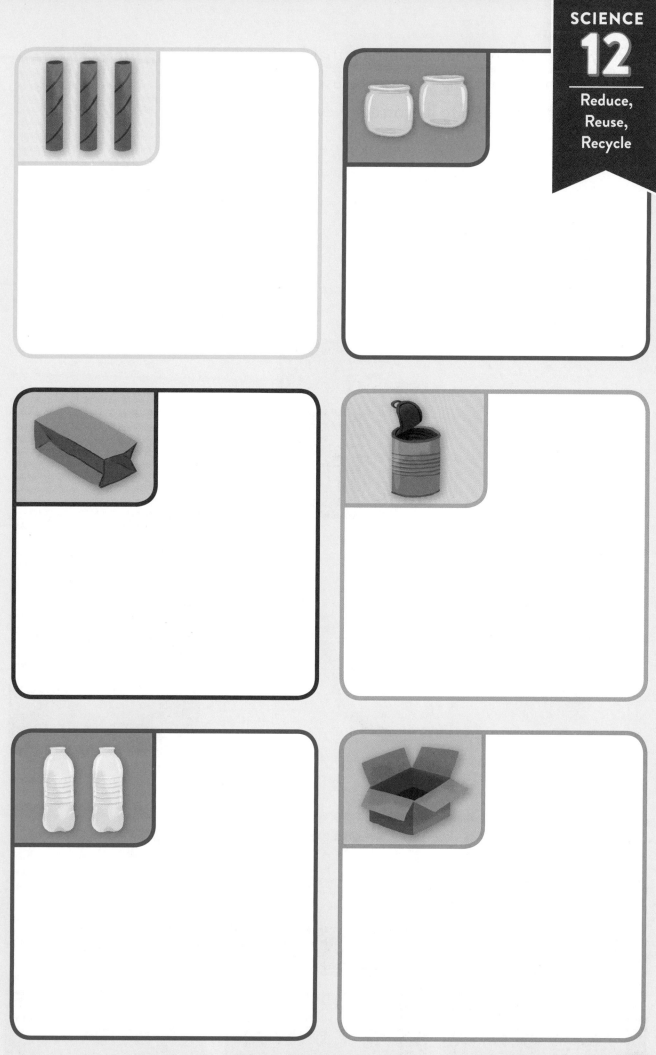

Recycling happens when something that has been used is changed into something that can be used again. Draw a line to connect each item to its correct recycling container.

Hunt for objects made of paper, glass, and metal in your home. Then, draw a picture of each one in the correct recycling container.

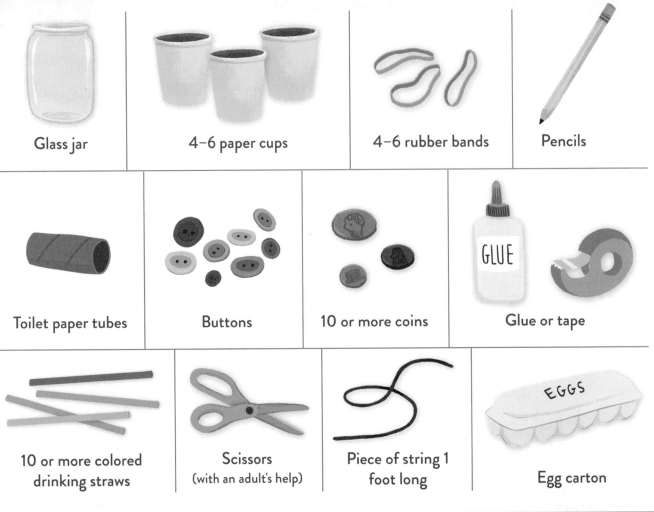

Glass jar	4–6 paper cups	4–6 rubber bands	Pencils
Toilet paper tubes	Buttons	10 or more coins	Glue or tape
10 or more colored drinking straws	Scissors (with an adult's help)	Piece of string 1 foot long	Egg carton

LET'S TINKER!

Stack, flip, connect, shake, tape, glue, or fit your materials inside of each other. What do they look like now? Can you imagine them as something else?

Make a new toy or item out of them.

224

LET'S MAKE: STRAW BRACELET!

1. Cut the straws into smaller pieces of different sizes.

2. Use them like beads on a piece of string!

What patterns and shapes can you make? What other materials can you add to the string?

3. Tie the string closed with a knot to make a bracelet.

LET'S ENGINEER!

Dimitri collects coins—lots of them. But he has nowhere to put them.

How can Dimitri store his coins using the materials around him?

Make a container to store coins in by reusing your materials. How can you use the materials to help you sort the different coins—pennies, nickels, dimes, and quarters—into piles? Are there any other materials in your home that you can reuse to help store the coins in?

PROJECT 12: DONE!
Get your sticker!

Pulls

You can move objects by pushing or pulling them. Circle the objects that are being pulled. Cross out the objects that are being pushed.

Push and pull your pencil! How does the pencil move when you push it away from yourself? When you pull it toward yourself?

Pulls can be of different strengths.
Circle the big pull. Cross out the little pull.

Draw something that you can pull in your home.

Can you give it a little pull? What about a big pull?

The MotMots are feeding the animals at the zoo. Circle each thing being pulled and draw an arrow in the direction of the pull.

Dimitri is pulling Enid on his sled. Write the numbers 1, 2, 3, and 4 to put the pictures in order of what happens first, second, third, and fourth.

Circle the things you pulled today.

Draw something else you pulled today.

LET'S START!

GATHER THESE TOOLS AND MATERIALS.

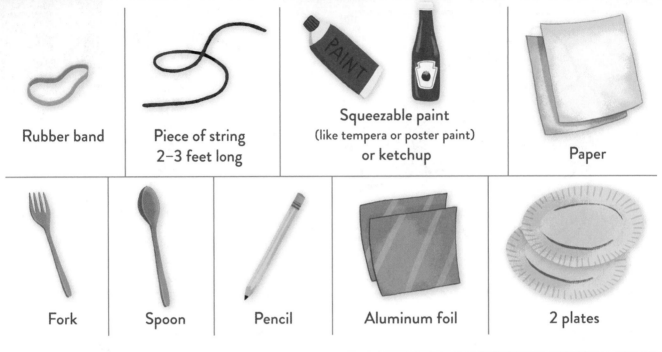

Rubber band	Piece of string 2–3 feet long	Squeezable paint (like tempera or poster paint) or ketchup	Paper
Fork	Spoon	Pencil	Aluminum foil	2 plates

LET'S TINKER!

Pull on the rubber band and then on the string. How are they different? Which one pulls more easily? Which is harder to pull and stretch?

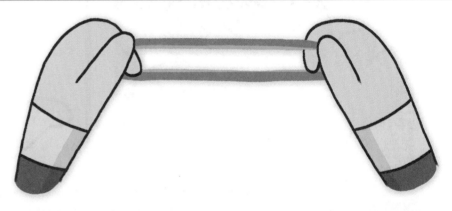

LET'S MAKE: PULL PAINTING!

1. **Squeeze** a small pile of paint (or ketchup) onto the middle of a piece of paper.

2. **Pull** different materials, like the fork, across the paint.

How do different materials affect the paint?

Which materials move the least paint?

Which ones move the most?

What happens when you pull the materials through the paint in a straight line? In zigzagging lines?

LET'S ENGINEER!

Enid has two baked potatoes, and Frank would like one. But it's too hot to touch!

How can Enid move one potato to Frank's plate?

Make a ball of foil to represent your potato.

Use a pull with one or more of your materials to move the foil ball from one plate to the other without touching the "potato" with your hands. Can you find more than one solution?

PROJECT 13: DONE!
Get your sticker!

Pushes

Pushing can make objects start moving. Draw the path that the watermelon takes when Brian pushes it down the hill to Amelia.

Can you push an object near you to make it start moving? Can you push the object again to make it stop moving?

Fill in what will happen when the MotMots push each object.

| bounce | roll | fall over | slide |

_____   _____

_____   _____

Sing this song aloud:

Push, push, push the boat gently down the stream. You might see a hungry pelican eating some ice cream.

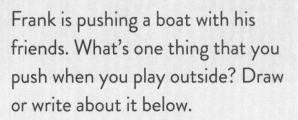

Frank is pushing a boat with his friends. What's one thing that you push when you play outside? Draw or write about it below.

Color each MotMot who is pushing something.

SCIENCE

14

Pushes

Pushes can be of different strengths. A bigger push can make an object go more quickly than a smaller push.

Circle the car that will move the fastest.

Circle the golf ball that will move the fastest.

Circle the bowling ball that will move the fastest.

Find an object that you can roll for your own experiment. It can be a ball, a toy car, or even a rolled-up sock! Set a start and a finish line.

Draw what happens when you give it a <u>little push</u>.

Draw what happens when you give it a <u>big push</u>.

Circle the winner!

LET'S START! GATHER THESE TOOLS AND MATERIALS.

Shoebox lid	Blocks or rocks	Paper	Drinking straw
Tape	Scissors (with an adult's help)	Markers	Cereal box (cut open and laid flat)

LET'S TINKER!

Put all your blocks or rocks in the shoebox lid. **Push** the lid. How does the lid move? Does it slide, roll, or tumble?

Now **stack** the blocks in one pile in the shoebox lid and push the lid. What happens? Can you push it without knocking over the blocks?

LET'S MAKE: AIR ROCKET!

1. Roll a small piece of paper (about the size of your palm) tightly around the end of a straw.

2. Tape the paper to make a tube.

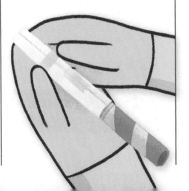

3. Fold the end of the tube and tape the folded part down.

4. Decorate your rocket by taping on small wings, fins, or a nose cone. You can also add stickers from page 387.

5. Blow quickly into the other end of the straw to watch the rocket fly!

LET'S ENGINEER!

Amelia's pet rabbit, Tuck, loves to play outside during the day and to play inside at night. But every time her pet rabbit wants to come inside or go outside, Amelia has to open the door.

How can Amelia make a door that her rabbit can easily open?

Using your cereal box as a wall, **create** a door that can open and close. Do you need to add anything so Tuck can push or pull the door?

PROJECT 14: DONE!
Get your sticker!

When two objects run into each other, they push on each other.
It's called a collision. Circle the objects that are colliding.

Snowball fight! Use the snowball stickers from page 387. Stick them where you want to aim your snowballs. Next, draw what will happen when your snowballs collide with these objects.

Sing this song aloud and act out the motions:

Head, shoulders, knees, and toes, knees and toes;

Head, shoulders, knees, and toes, knees and toes;

And eyes and ears and mouth and nose;

Head, shoulders, knees, and toes, knees and toes!

Collisions can stop an object, such as your hand, from moving. In this song, your hands collide with your body!

Collisions can also make objects move in different directions or at different speeds.

Draw what will happen when the bowling ball collides with the pins.

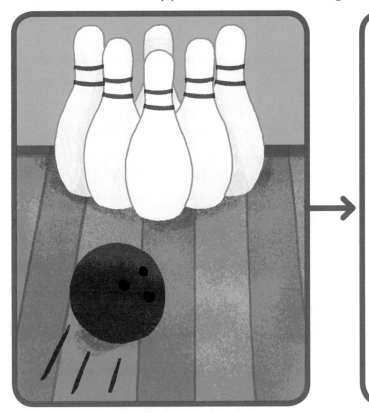 →

Draw what will happen when the water balloon collides with the target.

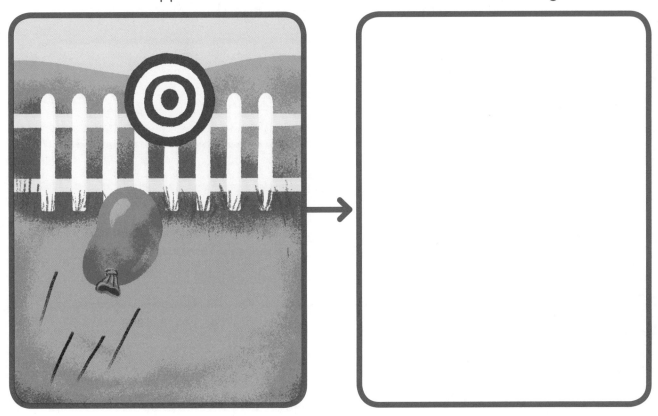 →

Clap quietly. Then clap louder. Write about what happens when your hands collide.

Toss one of your shoes at the other shoe. Write about what happens when your shoes collide.

Drop this book on the floor. Write about what happens when the book and the floor collide.

Give someone a high five. Write about what happens when your hands collide.

The bikes and fruits are about to collide! Draw arrows to show the directions the bikes and fruits are moving in.

LET'S START!

GATHER THESE TOOLS AND MATERIALS.

Pennies

Small objects like
rocks and cotton balls

Balls

Blocks

4–6 markers

Tights, sheer hose,
or long knee socks

LET'S TINKER!

Make a collision by pushing and pulling your materials together.

Try rolling, sliding, and dropping them, too. How does each react to a collision? Does it have the same reaction when you push or pull the object? How do the materials move differently on a table than on a carpet?

LET'S MAKE: PENNY PILEUP!

Collisions can make objects move. You can **make** a penny move without touching it!

1. Line up a bunch of pennies in a row. Each one should slightly overlap its neighbor.

2. Take another penny and quickly slide it so it collides with the end of the row.

What happens to the rest of the pennies? What happens if you slide the penny more gently? Harder? What happens if you slide two pennies into the row at the same time?

LET'S ENGINEER!

Amelia loves elephants—especially the way they knock down trees with their trunks. She wants to pretend to be an elephant, but she doesn't have a trunk.

How can she play pretend?

Stand the markers up on their caps, like tree trunks.

Put an object in one leg of the tights and let it dangle. Then hold it by your nose like it's an elephant's trunk. How can you make a collision with the markers?

PROJECT 15: DONE!
Get your sticker!

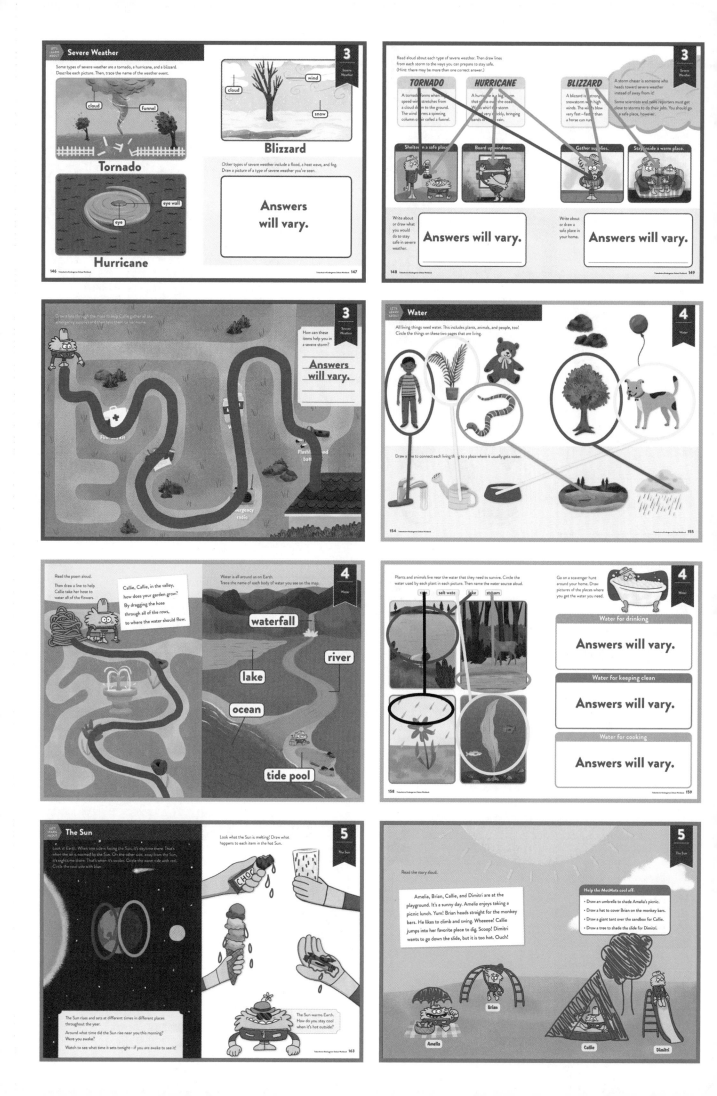

Severe Weather

Some types of severe weather are a tornado, a hurricane, and a blizzard. Describe each picture. Then, trace the name of the weather event.

cloud · funnel

Tornado

eye wall · eye

Hurricane

cloud · wind · snow

Blizzard

Other types of severe weather include a flood, a heat wave, and fog. Draw a picture of a type of severe weather you've seen.

Answers will vary.

Read aloud about each type of severe weather. Then draw lines from each storm to the ways you can prepare to stay safe.
(Hint: there may be more than one correct answer.)

TORNADO
A tornado forms when high speed wind stretches from a cloud down to the ground. The wind forms a spinning column of air called a funnel.

HURRICANE
A hurricane is a big storm that starts over the ocean. Winds whirl as the storm forms and very quickly, bringing bands of heavy rain.

BLIZZARD
A blizzard is a strong snowstorm with high winds. The winds blow very fast—faster than a horse can run.

A storm chaser is someone who heads toward severe weather instead of away from it!
Some scientists and news reporters must get close to storms to do their jobs. You should go to a safe place, however.

Shelter in a safe place. · Board up windows. · Gather supplies. · Stay inside a warm place.

Write about or draw what you would do to stay safe in severe weather.

Answers will vary.

Write about or draw a safe place in your home.

Answers will vary.

Draw a line through the maze to help Callie gather all the emergency supplies and then take them to her home.

First aid kit · Flashlight and batteries · Emergency radio

How can these items help you in a severe storm?

Answers will vary.

Water

All living things need water. This includes plants, animals, and people, too! Circle the things on these two pages that are living.

Draw a line to connect each living thing to a place where it usually gets water.

Read the poem aloud.

Then draw a line to help Callie take her hose to water all of the flowers.

Callie, Callie, in the valley, how does your garden grow? By dragging the hose through all of the rows, to where the water should flow.

Water is all around us on Earth. Trace the name of each body of water you see on the map.

waterfall · **river** · **lake** · **ocean** · **tide pool**

Plants and animals live near the water that they need to survive. Circle the water used by each plant in each picture. Then name the water source aloud.

rain · salt water · lake · stream

Go on a scavenger hunt around your home. Draw pictures of the places where you get the water you need.

Water for drinking

Answers will vary.

Water for keeping clean

Answers will vary.

Water for cooking

Answers will vary.

The Sun

Look at Earth. When one side is facing the Sun, it's daytime there. That's when the air is warmed by the Sun. On the other side, away from the Sun, it's nighttime there. That's when it's cooler. Circle the warm side with red. Circle the cool side with blue.

The Sun rises and sets at different times in different places throughout the year.
Around what time did the Sun rise near you this morning? Were you awake?
Watch to see what time it sets tonight—if you are awake to see it!

Look what the Sun is melting! Draw what happens to each item in the hot Sun.

CHOC

The Sun warms Earth. How do you stay cool when it's hot outside?

Read the story aloud.

Amelia, Brian, Callie, and Dimitri are at the playground. It's a sunny day. Amelia enjoys taking a picnic lunch. Yum! Brian heads straight for the monkey bars. He likes to climb and swing. Wheeee! Callie jumps into her favorite place to dig. Scoop! Dimitri wants to go down the slide, but it is too hot. Ouch!

Help the MotMots cool off!
· Draw an umbrella to shade Amelia's picnic.
· Draw a hat to cover Brian on the monkey bars.
· Draw a giant tent over the sandbox for Callie.
· Draw a tree to shade the slide for Dimitri.

Amelia · Brian · Callie · Dimitri

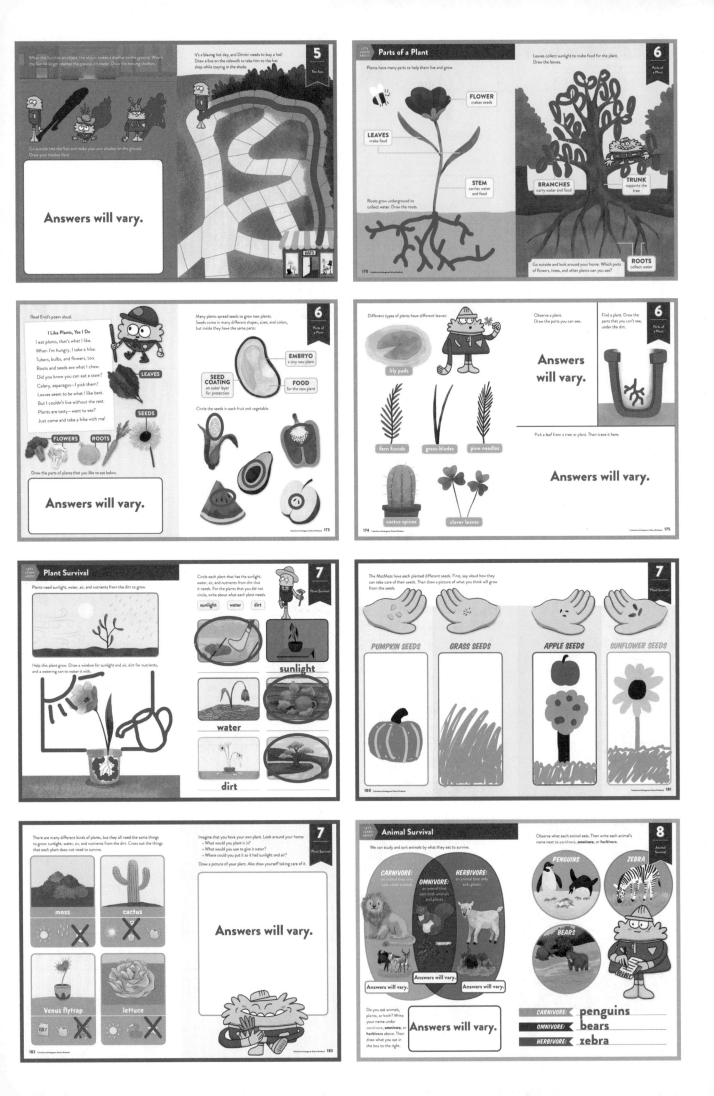

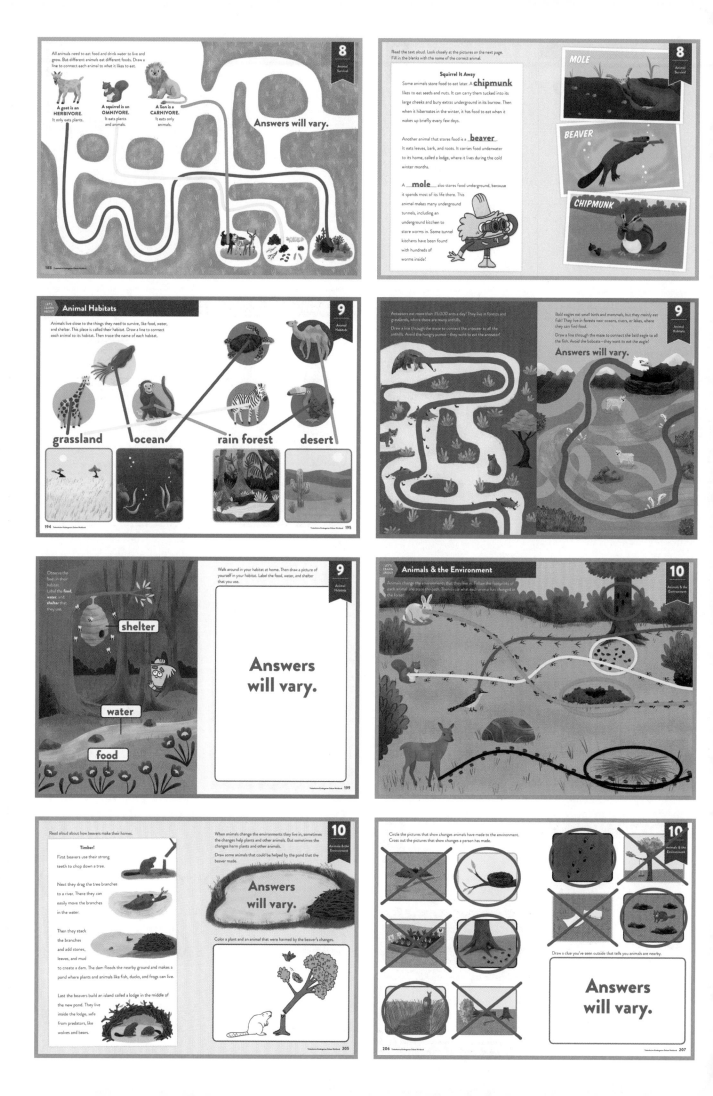

Page 8 (Animal Survival)

All animals need to eat food and drink water to live and grow. But different animals eat different foods. Draw a line to connect each animal to what it likes to eat.

A goat is an **HERBIVORE.** It only eats plants.

A squirrel is an **OMNIVORE.** It eats plants and animals.

A lion is a **CARNIVORE.** It eats only animals.

Answers will vary.

Read the text aloud. Look closely at the pictures on the next page. Fill in the blanks with the name of the correct animal.

Squirrel It Away

Some animals store food to eat later. A **chipmunk** likes to eat seeds and nuts. It can carry them tucked into its large cheeks and bury extras underground in its burrow. Then when it hibernates in the winter, it has food to eat when it wakes up briefly every few days.

Another animal that stores food is a **beaver**. It eats leaves, bark, and roots. It carries food underwater to its home, called a lodge, where it lives during the cold winter months.

A **mole** also stores food underground, because it spends most of its life there. This animal makes many underground tunnels, including an underground kitchen to store worms in. Some tunnel kitchens have been found with hundreds of worms inside!

MOLE

BEAVER

CHIPMUNK

Page 9 — Animal Habitats

Animals live close to the things they need to survive, like food, water, and shelter. This place is called their habitat. Draw a line to connect each animal to its habitat. Then trace the name of each habitat.

grassland   ocean   rain forest   desert

Anteaters eat more than 35,000 ants a day! They live in forests and grasslands, where there are many anthills.

Draw a line through the maze to connect the anteater to all the anthills. Avoid the hungry pumas—they want to eat the anteater!

Bald eagles eat small birds and mammals, but they mainly eat fish! They live in forests near oceans, rivers, or lakes, where they can find food.

Draw a line through the maze to connect the bald eagle to all the fish. Avoid the bobcats—they want to eat the eagle!

Answers will vary.

Observe the bees in their habitat. Label the **food**, **water**, and **shelter** that they use.

shelter

water

food

Walk around in your habitat at home. Then draw a picture of yourself in your habitat. Label the food, water, and shelter that you use.

Answers will vary.

Page 10 — Animals & the Environment

Animals change the environments that they live in. Follow the footprints of each animal and trace the path. Then circle what each animal has changed in the forest.

Read aloud about how beavers make their homes.

Timber!

First beavers use their strong teeth to chop down a tree.

Next they drag the tree branches to a river. There they can easily move the branches in the water.

Then they stack the branches and add stones, leaves, and mud to create a dam. The dam floods the nearby ground and makes a pond where plants and animals like fish, ducks, and frogs can live.

Last the beavers build an island called a lodge in the middle of the new pond. They live inside the lodge, safe from predators, like wolves and bears.

When animals change the environments they live in, sometimes the changes help plants and other animals. But sometimes the changes harm plants and other animals.

Draw some animals that could be helped by the pond that the beaver made.

Answers will vary.

Color a plant and an animal that were harmed by the beaver's changes.

Circle the pictures that show changes animals have made to the environment. Cross out the pictures that show changes a person has made.

Draw a clue you've seen outside that tells you animals are nearby.

Answers will vary.

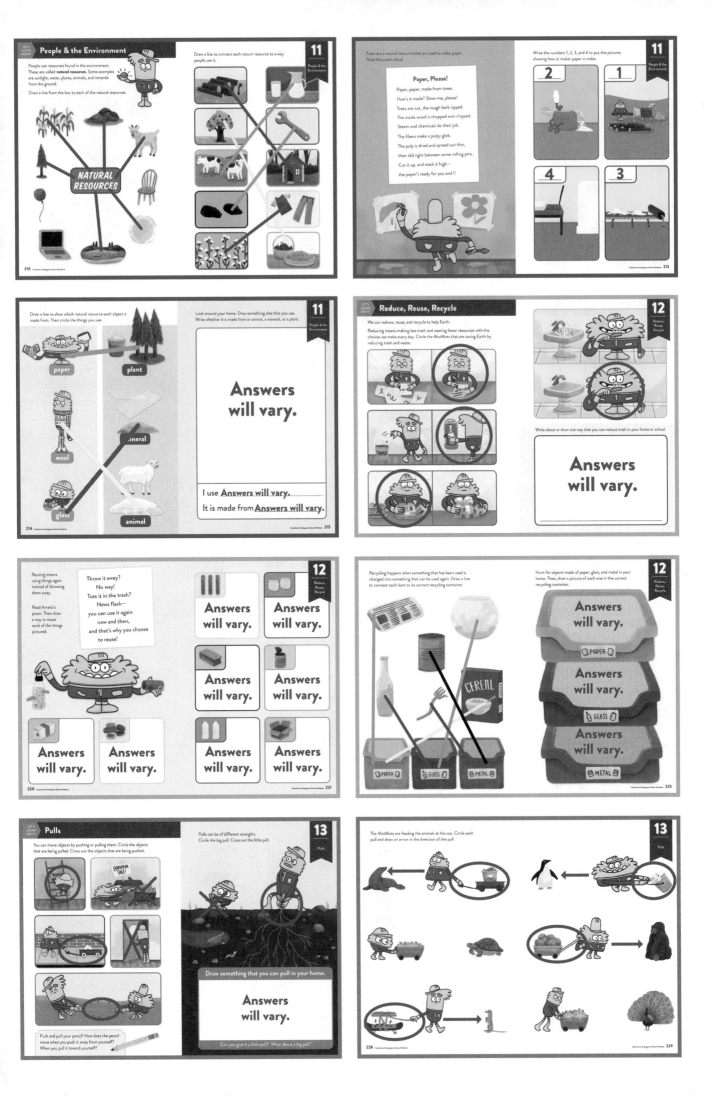

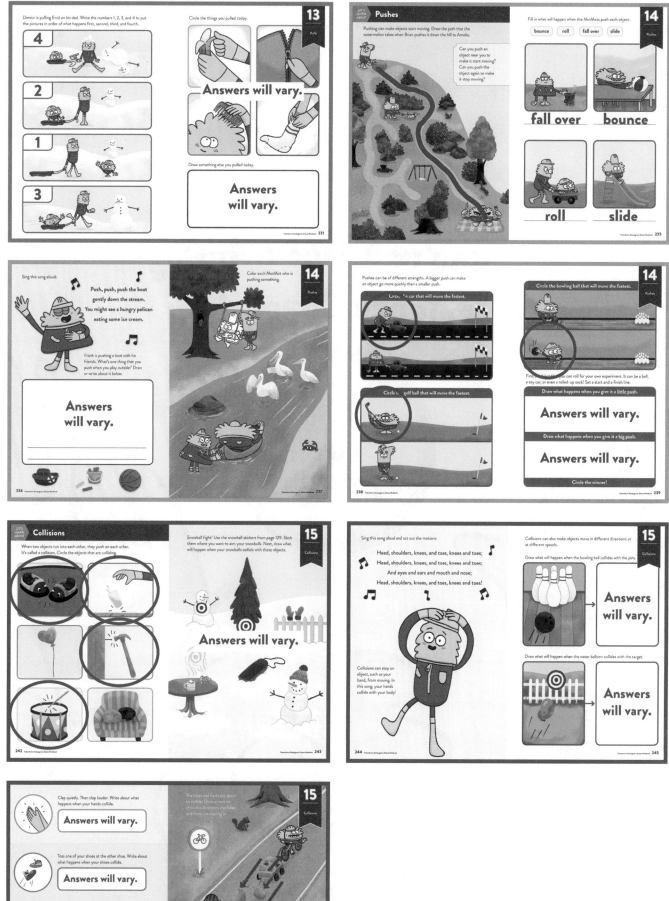

Dimitri is pulling Enid on his sled. Write the numbers 1, 2, 3, and 4 to put the pictures in order of what happens first, second, third, and fourth.

4

2

1

3

Circle the things you pulled today.

Answers will vary.

Draw something else you pulled today.

Answers will vary.

Pushes

Pushing can make objects start moving. Draw the path that the watermelon takes when Brian pushes it down the hill to Amelia.

Can you push an object near you to make it start moving? Can you push the object again to make it stop moving?

Fill in what will happen when the MotMots push each object.

bounce   roll   fall over   slide

fall over   **bounce**

roll   **slide**

Sing this song aloud:

Push, push, push the boat gently down the stream. You might see a hungry pelican eating some ice cream.

Frank is pushing a boat with his friends. What's one thing that you push when you play outside? Draw or write about it below.

Answers will vary.

Color each MotMot who is pushing something.

Pushes can be of different strengths. A bigger push can make an object go more quickly than a smaller push.

Circle the car that will move the fastest.

Circle the golf ball that will move the fastest.

Circle the bowling ball that will move the fastest.

Find an object that you can roll for your own experiment. It can be a ball, a toy car, or even a rolled-up sock! Set a start and a finish line.

Draw what happens when you give it a little push.

Answers will vary.

Draw what happens when you give it a big push.

Answers will vary.

Circle the winner!

Collisions

When two objects run into each other, they push on each other. It's called a collision. Circle the objects that are colliding.

Snowball fight! Use the snowball stickers from page 129. Stick them where you want to aim your snowballs. Next, draw what will happen when your snowballs collide with these objects.

Answers will vary.

Sing this song aloud and act out the motions:

Head, shoulders, knees, and toes, knees and toes! Head, shoulders, knees, and toes, knees and toes; And eyes and ears and mouth and nose; Head, shoulders, knees, and toes, knees and toes!

Collisions can stop an object, such as your hand, from moving. In this song, your hands collide with your body!

Collisions can also make objects move in different directions or at different speeds.

Draw what will happen when the bowling ball collides with the pins.

Answers will vary.

Draw what will happen when the water balloon collides with the target.

Answers will vary.

Clap quietly. Then clap louder. Write about what happens when your hands collide.

Answers will vary.

Toss one of your shoes at the other shoe. Write about what happens when your shoes collide.

Answers will vary.

Drop this book on the floor. Write about what happens when the book and the floor collide.

Answers will vary.

Give someone a high five. Write about what happens when your hands collide.

Answers will vary.

The bikes and fruits are about to collide. Draw arrows to show the directions the bikes and fruits are moving in.

TinkerActive WORKBOOKS

KINDERGARTEN · ENGLISH LANGUAGE ARTS · AGES 5–6

by Megan Hewes Butler

illustrated by Bronwyn Gruet

educational consulting by Randi House

 Odd Dot · New York

The Alphabet

With the help of an adult, read the poem aloud. Then circle a food that you would like to eat.

Today we're cooking **Alphabet Soup**.

Here's the recipe to make this goop:

Apples, **b**utter, then some **c**heese,

Or start with **d**oughnuts if you please.

Stir in some **e**ggs, **f**igs, and **g**rapes,

Then some **h**am cut into shapes.

Ice cream and **j**elly go on top,

Kiwi and **l**emon get a chop.

Milk and **n**oodles go in slow—

Add **o**nions and **p**eas, and cook on low.

Quark is a cheese that starts with Q,

Toss in some **r**aisins and **s**alt, too.

Add **t**urnips and **u**don noodles, please,

Vinegar and **w**affles are the keys.

Next comes **x**igua—melon from a vine.

A scoop of **y**ogurt will taste fine.

We'll be finished cooking soon,

Add chopped **z**ucchini and grab a spoon!

Draw a line from A to Z in alphabetical order, and read each letter aloud.

Say the name of each food aloud. Listen for the sound at the start of the word. Then trace the uppercase and lowercase letters.

apple
Aa

butter
Bb

cake
Cc

figs
Ff

grapes
Gg

ham
Hh

lemon
Ll

milk
Mm

noodles
Nn

quark
Qq

raisins
Rr

salt
Ss

vinegar
Vv

waffles
Ww

xigua
Xx

doughnut

D d

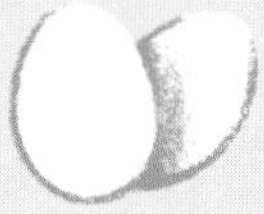

eggs

E e

ice cream

I i

jelly

J j

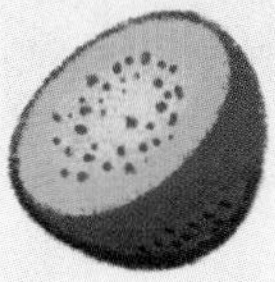

kiwi

K k

onion

O o

peas

P p

turnip

T t

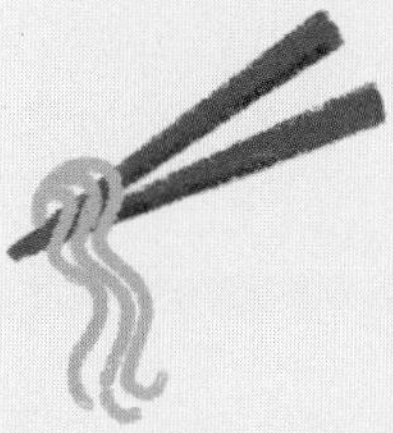

udon

U u

yogurt

Y y

zucchini

Z z

A, E, I, O, and U are vowels. Circle the five ingredients that start with vowels.

Draw a line to match each uppercase and lowercase letter.

Write your name, and then say the sound that each letter makes. Hunt for objects around your home that start with each letter in your name. Then draw pictures of your objects.

F r a n k

flag   rabbit   ape   nose   key

LET'S START!

GATHER THESE TOOLS AND MATERIALS.

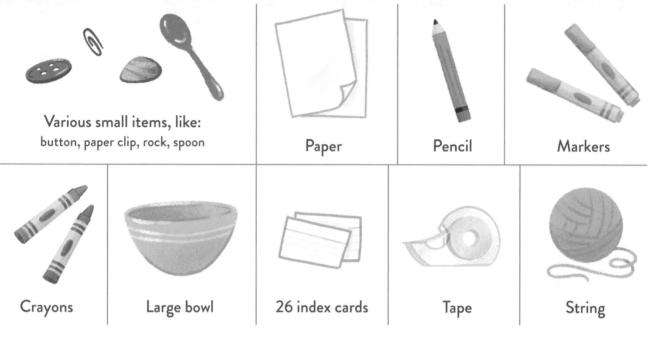

Various small items, like:
button, paper clip, rock, spoon

Paper

Pencil

Markers

Crayons

Large bowl

26 index cards

Tape

String

LET'S TINKER!

Hold up each of your materials one at a time. **Say** the name aloud. Which letter does each object start with? **Say** the letter aloud. Do any of the materials start with the same letter? Do any of the materials start with the same letter as your name?

LET'S MAKE: ALPHABET SALAD!

1. Write your name with a pencil on a piece of paper.

2. Find an ingredient in your kitchen that starts with each letter in your name.

3. Draw the ingredient under each letter in your name using crayons or markers.

4. With the help of an adult, **combine** the ingredients in a large bowl to make your alphabet salad.

LET'S ENGINEER!

The MotMots are making banners for an Alphabet Parade, but they keep mixing up the order of the letters of the alphabet.

How can they keep the letters in the correct order?

Get your stack of 26 index cards. **Write** one letter of the alphabet on each card. **Lay** the cards in order from A to Z. How can you check that your cards are in the correct order? How can you keep the letters in place? **Find** all the vowels. How can you decorate the vowel cards to stand out?

PROJECT 1: DONE!
Get your sticker!

A **science fiction** story is made up about a world where science plays a big part. There can be spaceships, time travel, or even creatures from other planets! With the help of an adult, read this science fiction story aloud.

The Rocket

"Come on up!" called Frank from the tree fort.

Amelia tried to grab the rope ladder, but she couldn't reach it. Then her foot slipped and she fell—ouch! Amelia rubbed her knee— she had bumped into something hot. What was it?

Amelia picked up a small gem from the ground. It was glowing red and felt warm. She wiped some dirt off the shiny surface. Did the gem flash? A humming noise made Amelia look up. A rocket was slowly landing next to her!

The door opened and Amelia peeked inside, where she saw a dark wall of buttons. A friendly computer voice said, "I'll take you anywhere you want to go. Just say the name so I will know." The rocket could talk! And it would take her anywhere! Where should she go? Amelia's mind raced. To the zoo? A magic show? A castle? To the moon? She couldn't decide. Amelia looked around for Frank.

When she turned back again, the rocket was gone. Her shoulders slumped as she thought about the adventure she didn't get to take. Then she realized that her hand felt warm. There, still in her hand, was the glowing red gem.

Look at each picture from the story and say the name aloud.
Then write each word.

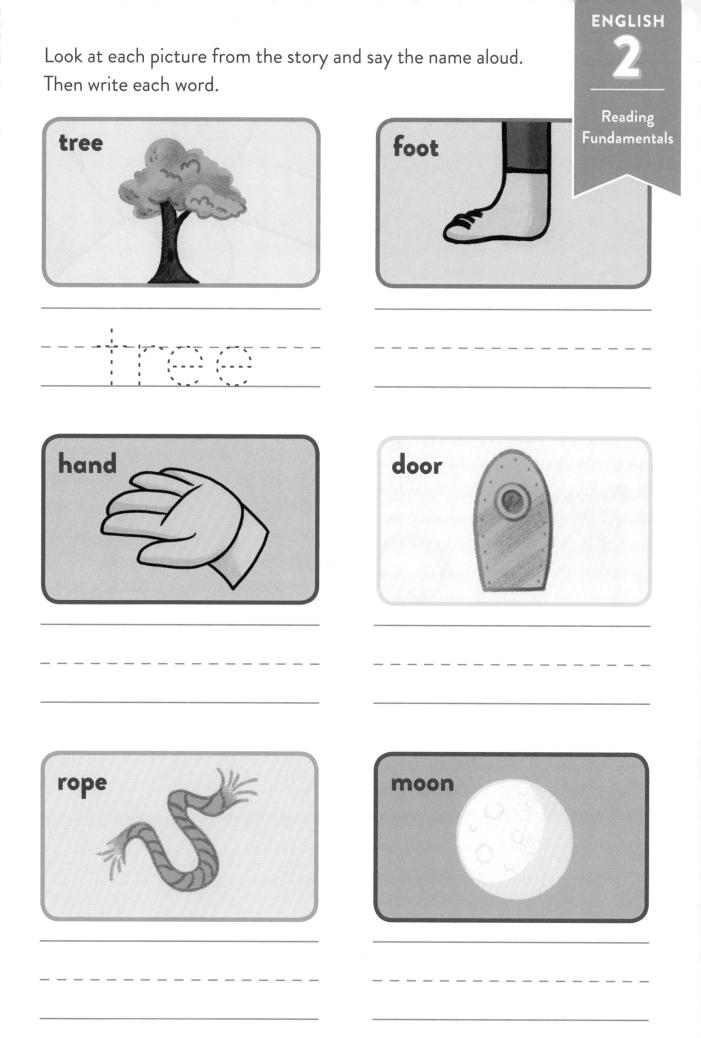

tree

foot

- - - tree - - -

hand

door

rope

moon

Amelia discovered a hidden gem. It was red and shiny.

Circle the other objects that are **red**.

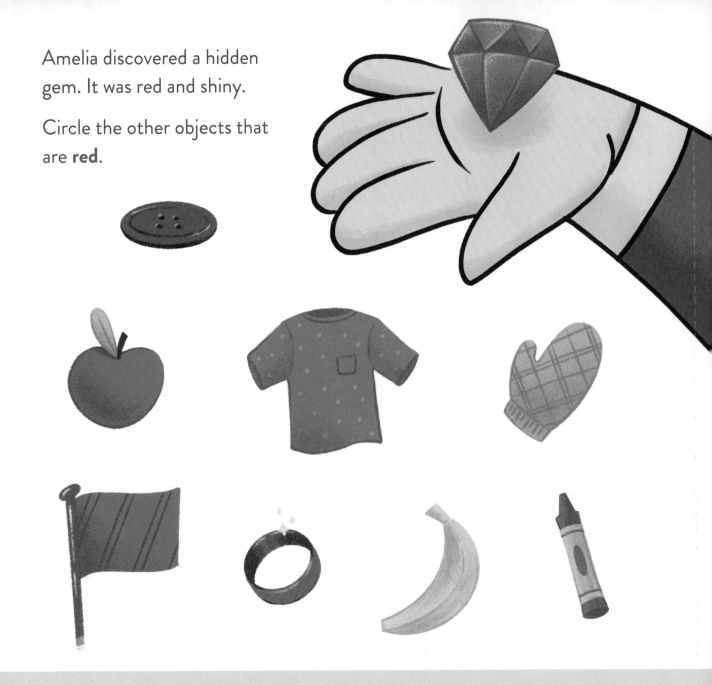

Look around you. Write about or draw something that is shiny.

Drag your finger on the rocket's trail as you read the sentences aloud.

Amelia saw a rocket.

→

Read from left to right.
At the end of each line,
move down to the next
line, and read from left
to right again.

She told Frank.

Frank did not see the rocket.

Draw the path of the rocket from left to right as you read each sentence aloud.

Amelia held the gem.

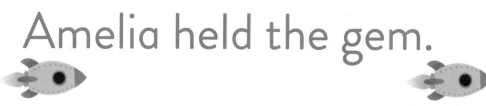

The gem was warm.

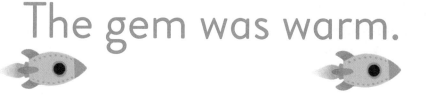

The gem began to glow!

Complete each sentence. If you write more than one word, place one finger between the words to leave spaces. When you're done writing, draw rocket trails to show how to follow the words in the sentences above.

scared

happy

If I saw a rocket, I would be _____.

the stars

the ocean

If I could fly the rocket, I would go to _____.

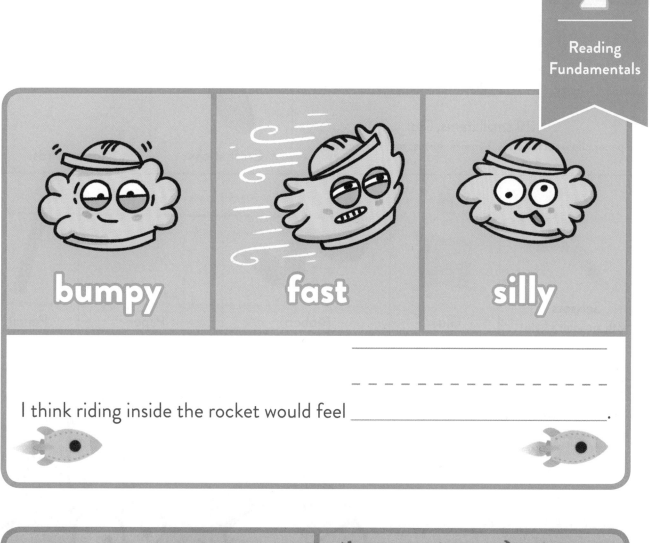

bumpy   fast   silly

I think riding inside the rocket would feel _____.

look around   have a party

When I got there, I'd _____.

LET'S START!

GATHER THESE TOOLS AND MATERIALS.

20 small items, like:
paper clips, cotton balls, pennies, beans, pebbles, buttons

Craft sticks

Index cards

Scissors
(with an adult's help)

Glue

Ribbon

Paper

Pencil

LET'S TINKER!

Line up a handful of your materials in a row. **Make** spaces in between each item, just like the spaces in between words in a sentence. **Point** at each object in the row and say the name aloud. Can you follow the objects moving from left to right, just like when you are reading? **Try** adding objects and starting another line below.

LET'S MAKE: ROCKET READER!

1. Glue 3 craft sticks onto an index card to make the body of the rocket.

2. Cut off the extra paper on the sides. **Trim** the top into a triangle shape for the top of the rocket.

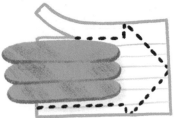

3. Glue pieces of ribbon to the bottom of the rocket.

4. Once it is dry, **decorate** the rocket. You can **use** stickers from page 389.

5. Use your rocket as a pointing stick for reading. **Get** your favorite book and point at each word in a sentence as you read it aloud. **Move** your rocket down to the next line when you're at the end. You can also **use** your rocket as a bookmark!

LET'S ENGINEER!

The MotMots love that rockets are fast and lightweight and that they can fly. They want to play with more things like rockets.

How can the MotMots find other toys like rockets?

Take 3 pieces of paper and write 1 rocket description on each: fast / lightweight / can fly. **Search** your home for other things that share these qualities and lay them on each piece of paper. (If the item is too large, you can draw it on the paper instead.) Can you find an item that you can put on all 3 pieces of paper? It's fast, lightweight, and able to fly?

fast

lightweight

can fly

PROJECT 2: DONE!
Get your sticker!

With the help of an adult, read the newspaper article aloud.

The Tinker Town News

Farmer Fim Gets a New Yak

Farmer Fim has the largest farm in town. At the diner this morning he shared some big news. Yesterday he brought a new animal to his farm—a yak! He already has many animals, including a cat, a dog, a fox, a cow, a pig, a hen, and even a rat. But now he is building a special pen on his farm for his newest animal, the yak.

The new yak has long brown fur. She also has horns and thick fat to keep her warm in cold weather. The yak lives in a field full of grass, which she eats. The farm will now sell yak milk, yak butter, and yak cheese! Some of the people in the diner could not wait to try these foods. Other people were not so sure.

Read the name of each animal aloud. Then draw a line to connect each animal to the correct stall and write the missing vowel.

hen

pig

yak

cow

c __ w   p __ g   h __ n   y __ k

Trace each word and say the sound each letter makes, like this: p - i - g.

pig   mud   pen

fox   log   den

Use your hands, your arms, or your whole body to make the shape of each letter!

bat   nap

Look at each picture and say the name of each animal aloud.
Then circle the correct name.

cat   bat

bug   dog

cub   cow

pig   pup

hog   hen

rat   rabbit

Vowels can make different sounds.

Long vowels sound just like their letter names.

whale   **bee**   **mice**   **mole**   **mule**

Short vowels make a different sound.

yak   **hen**   **pig**   **fox**   **bug**

a Circle the objects that have a **long a** sound.

e Circle the objects that have a **short e** sound.

i These action words all have the **short i** sound.
Draw a picture of yourself doing each action.

spin

tip

skid

o Hunt around your home for these objects with a **short o** sound:

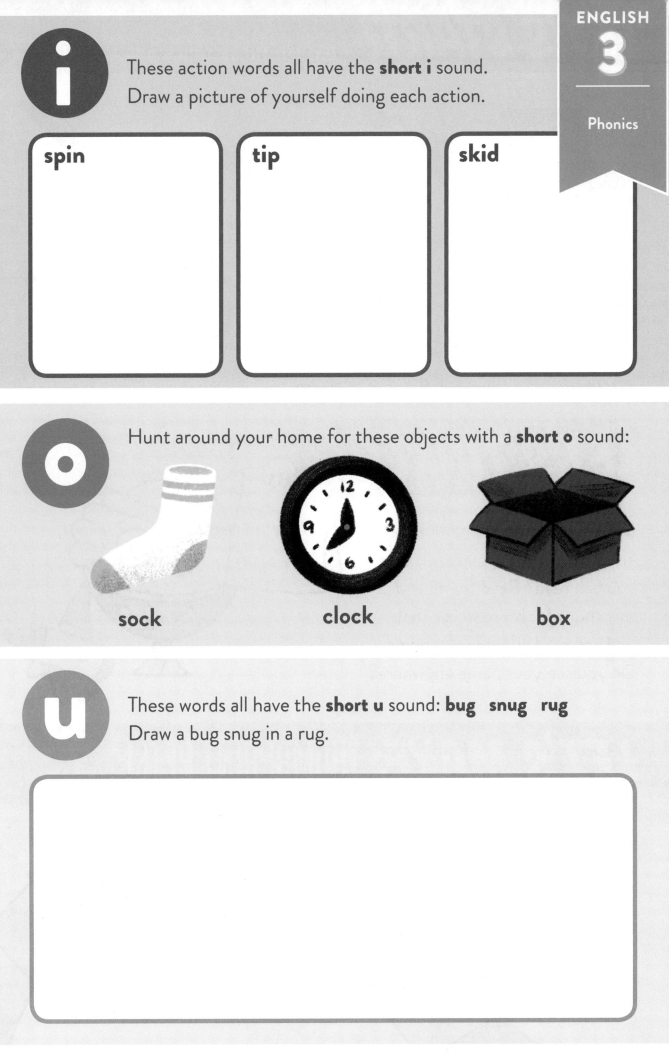

sock

clock

box

u These words all have the **short u** sound: **bug   snug   rug**
Draw a bug snug in a rug.

LET'S START!

GATHER THESE TOOLS AND MATERIALS.

Ink pad or paint

Paper

Pen

Markers

Index cards

Crayons

String

Paper clips

LET'S TINKER!

Look at your materials. Are there any words on your materials that you can read? **Read** them, and then hunt for more words that you can read around your home. Do you see your name anywhere?

CAT FOOD

LET'S MAKE: THUMBPRINT PETS!

1. **Press** your thumb into the ink pad and place it on a piece of paper. (If you are using paint, put a small amount in a container and do the same action.) **Let** your thumbprint dry.

2. **Use** a pen or marker to add details to the thumbprint, like legs, eyes, or a tail, to create your own pet.

3. Make a short vowel pet, like a bug, bat, or yak. Then **make** a long vowel pet, like a spider, bee, or goat!

LET'S ENGINEER!

Farmer Fim wants to welcome new animals to his farm. He always hangs a sign for each animal over its stall in the barn. But his sign maker is broken! He only has these letters in his shed: P G C T W I A O.

How can Farmer Fim welcome new animals with the letters he has?

Write each letter below on a different index card. **Move** the cards around to see if you can spell animal names. Which animals can you spell? Are there any that you cannot spell? Which letters are you missing? **Hang** your signs.

P
G
I
T
C
W
A
O

PROJECT 3: DONE!
Get your sticker!

With the help of an adult, read the play aloud. Then act out the play in your own words. Use different voices for each character!

Going on Vacation

GIRL: I went on the best trip—I went to a hot beach!

BOY: Really? I like the cold snow better.

GIRL: But what about swimming slowly in the waves?

BOY: I like to slide fast on a sled!

GIRL: But what about building small sandcastles?

BOY: I like to build big snowmen.

GIRL: We like opposite things.

BOY: But we both like to go on trips!

You can be an actor in a play! Read each action word and then act it out.

lean	wiggle	flop

Circle the action above that made you move the most.

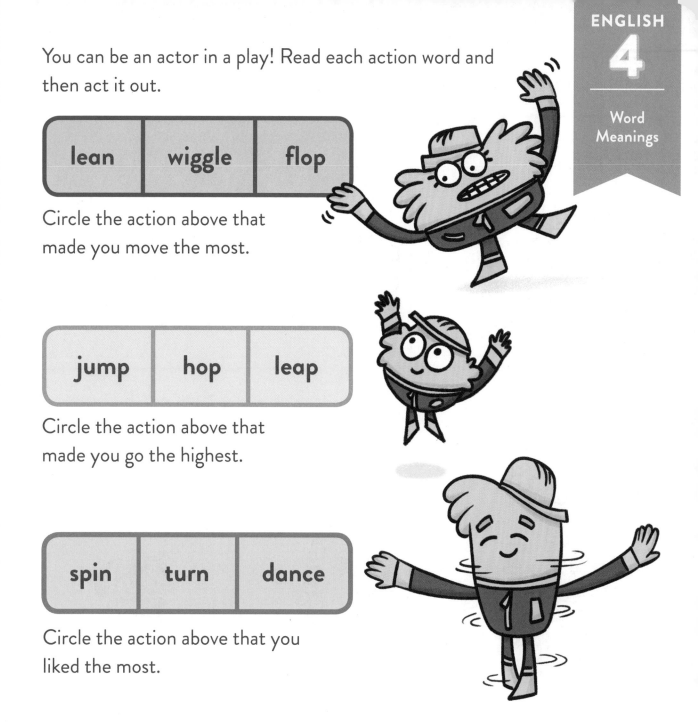

jump	hop	leap

Circle the action above that made you go the highest.

spin	turn	dance

Circle the action above that you liked the most.

Draw a picture of yourself doing your favorite action.

Antonyms are words that mean the opposite of each other. Read each word aloud and look at the picture. Then circle the antonym.

sleeping

sitting

frowning

Act it out! What is an antonym of standing still?

Synonyms are words that have almost the same meaning.
Read each group of words and circle the synonyms.

fast   quick   late

glad   mad   happy

loud   silly   noisy

sad   sleepy   tired

Act it out! What is a synonym of giggling?

Words that **rhyme** have the same middle and ending sound, like hop and stop. Read the names of the three objects in each row. Then circle the two words that rhyme.

nail   tree   snail

spring   moon   spoon

cake   snake   bag

mouse   can   house

Draw a picture of another word that rhymes with each set.

Cat rhymes with bat.

Van rhymes with can.

Bug rhymes with hug.

Dried beans	Index cards	Crayons	Rubber bands

Small items, like:
buttons, cotton balls, twist ties, paper clips, small toys

Jars

Toilet paper tube

LET'S TINKER!

Read this rhyme aloud:

I know a word that rhymes with BEANS.
Listen close: the word is JEANS!

Pick up one of your materials and use your own words to continue the rhyme:

I know a word that rhymes
with _____.

Listen close: the word
is _____!

How many materials can you rhyme? **Hunt** around your home for objects that you can rhyme your materials with.

LET'S MAKE: JUMPING BEAN GAME!

1. Get 6 index cards. On each card, **draw** an action you can do with beans. For example, hold one bean up high, hold some beans and run fast, etc.

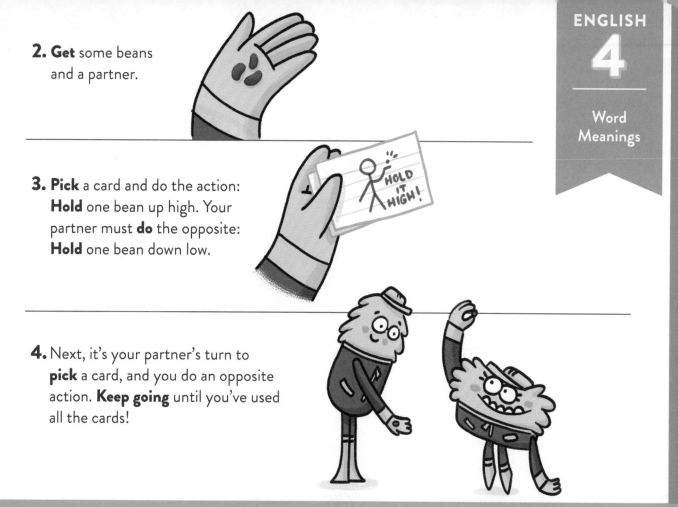

2. Get some beans
and a partner.

3. Pick a card and do the action:
Hold one bean up high. Your
partner must **do** the opposite:
Hold one bean down low.

4. Next, it's your partner's turn to
pick a card, and you do an opposite
action. **Keep going** until you've used
all the cards!

LET'S ENGINEER!

All the MotMots loved the play. But Callie has never swum slowly, and Brian has never slid fast on a sled—so they weren't exactly sure why they were opposites.

How can Callie and Brian teach each other about these opposites?

Use your materials to build models of opposites. Can you make these opposites from the play?

- slow and fast
- small and big

What other opposites can you make models of?

PROJECT 4: DONE!
Get your sticker!

Word Building

Nursery rhymes are poems that often tell stories. Some can even be sung like songs. With the help of an adult, read this nursery rhyme aloud.

One, two, three, four, five.

Once I caught a fish alive.

Six, seven, eight, nine, ten.

Then I let it go again.

Why did you let it go?

Because it bit my finger so.

Which finger did it bite?

This little finger on my right.

The words **five** and **alive** rhyme. Read the poem again and draw a circle around the words at the end of the lines that rhyme with each other.

Look at each picture. Then circle the matching word.

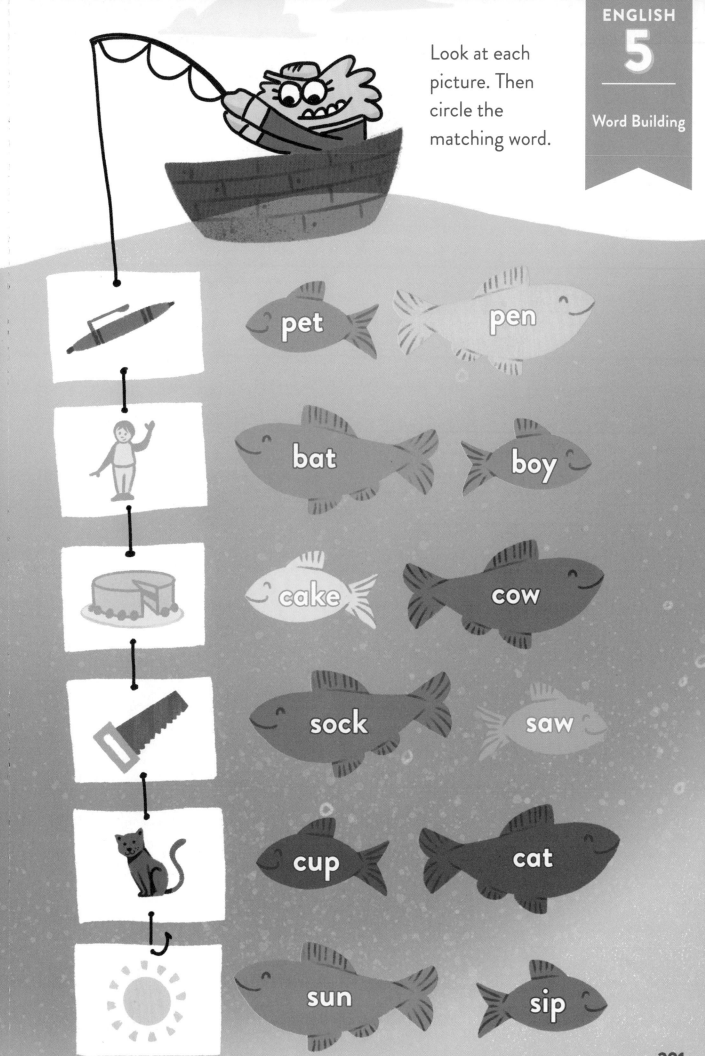

pet   pen

bat   boy

cake   cow

sock   saw

cup   cat

sun   sip

Count each group of ocean animals aloud. If there is more than one animal in each group, trace the word and add an **s** to make it plural.

shark _____

whale _____

eel _____

oyster _____

crab _____

clam _____

Count each group of objects aloud. If there is more than one object in each group, trace the word and add **es** to make it plural.

bush _____

bench _____

bus _____

lunch _____

peach _____

Words that end in **-s**, **-sh**, **-ch**, **-x**, or **-z** become plural when you add **-es**.

Fill in the missing letter in each word. Then say the words aloud.

s b h

___it   ___it   ___it

c v p

___an   ___an   ___an

d j l

___og   ___og   ___og

Fill in the missing vowel in each word. Then say the words aloud.

a   i   e

t ___ n   t ___ n   t ___ n

a   o   u

h ___ t   h ___ t   h ___ t

u   a   o

c ___ p   c ___ p   c ___ p

LET'S START!

GATHER THESE TOOLS AND MATERIALS.

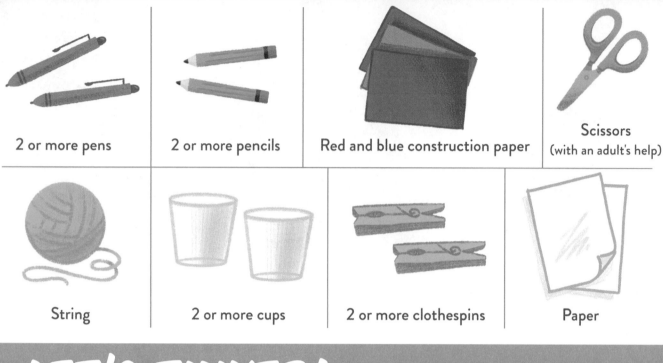

2 or more pens	2 or more pencils
Red and blue construction paper	Scissors (with an adult's help)
String	2 or more cups
2 or more clothespins	Paper

LET'S TINKER!

Pick up one tool or material and say the name aloud. Then **pick** up another of the same tool or material, count the group, and then say the name aloud. How has the word changed in going from singular (for one material) to plural (for two materials)? Does the name change if you pick up three materials, or four? Do any of the names not change when there are more than one?

Pens!

Pen

LET'S MAKE: FISHING FOR WORDS!

1. Cut 4 small squares of red paper and write these letters: N, R, T, L.

2. Cut 3 small squares of blue paper and write these pairs of letters: AP, IP, OT.

3. Fold each piece of paper in half and put it in a cup.

4. Go fishing with a clothespin. **Pull** out 1 red paper and 1 blue paper.

5. Lay the papers down to spell a word. **Read** it aloud, then go fishing again!

LET'S ENGINEER!

The MotMots are trying to see who can spell the most words that end in -at. Each word is worth one point, and the MotMot with the most points wins!

How can Callie make sure she spells all the words that end in -at?

Get a pencil and paper. How can you try all the possible combinations? **Give** yourself 1 point for each word!

PROJECT 5: DONE!
Get your sticker!

Vocabulary

A **map** is a drawing that shows where things are. With the help of an adult, read the map.

Prepositions are words that can describe where something is located or what direction it is going.

Read the sentences below. Then draw and use stickers from page 389 to add details to the map.

Brian rode his bike **through** the park **from** his house **to** school. Draw his path using a **blue** crayon.

Circle the dog that Brian rode by **on** his bike ride **to** school using an **orange** crayon.

Next, his class rode a school bus **around** the pond **to** the fire station. Draw their path using a **yellow** crayon.

There was a fire truck parked **in** the parking lot **behind** the fire station. Use a sticker from page 389 to add the truck.

Across from the fire station there was a cat stuck **in** a tree! Use a sticker from page 389 to add the cat.

Circle the flag that flies **above** the fire station using a **red** crayon.

Draw what you think Brian saw **inside** the fire station.

These question words can be used to find out more information: **who**, **what**, **where**, **when**, **why**, and **how**.

Read each question, and circle the answer.

What did Brian ride to school?

fire truck   bike

Where did Brian go on his field trip?

fire station   school

When did Brian go to the fire station?

during the day   at night

Who do you think Brian met on his field trip?

police officer   firefighter

What do you want to ask about Brian's field trip? Use a question word to start your sentence.

Read each question and answer. Then fill in the missing word at the beginning of each question.

Why   What

Q: _____ is your clothing called?

A: Our protective clothing is called bunker gear. It helps protect us.

How   When

Q: _____ much does your gear weigh?

A: Our gear usually weighs more than a kindergartner!

What   Why

Q: _____ are there different types of fire vehicles?

A: Different vehicles help us do different jobs. Fire engines pump water. Fire trucks carry ladders and tools.

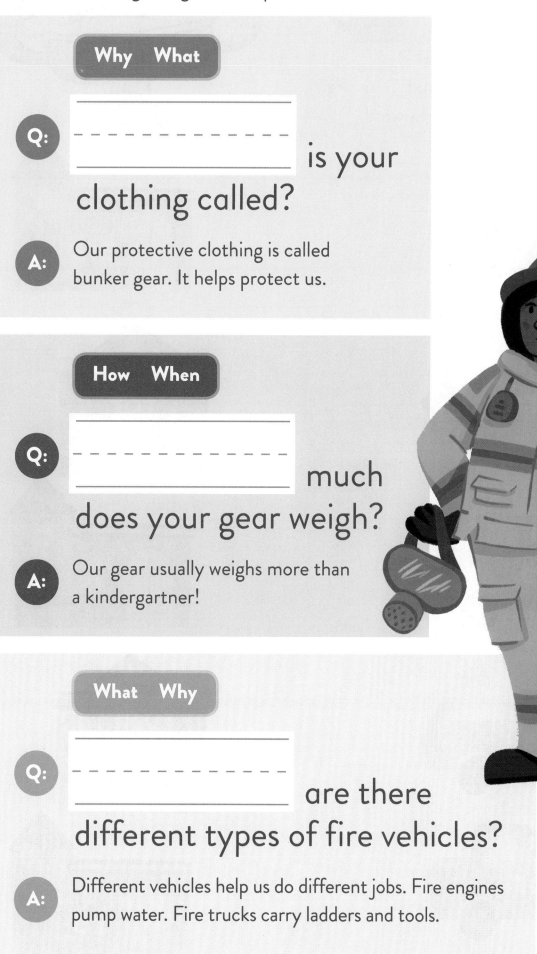

Sight words are common words that good readers memorize to help them read.

Read each sight word aloud. Then draw a line to the matching sight word.

the

are

to

is

for

are

for

is

the

to

Color the water **blue**. Color the curtains **yellow**.
Color the building **orange**. Color the smoke **black**.
Color the fire truck **red**. Color the light on the stoplight **green**.

LET'S START!

GATHER THESE TOOLS AND MATERIALS.

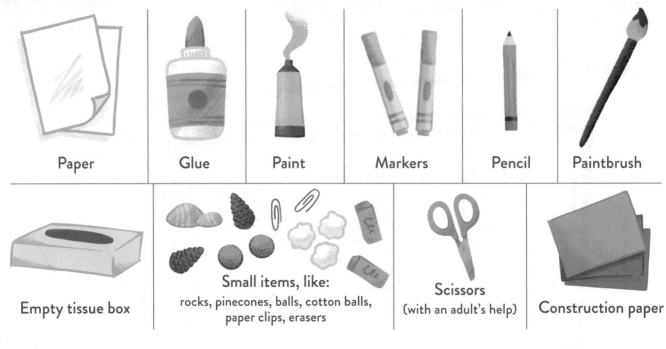

| Paper | Glue | Paint | Markers | Pencil | Paintbrush |

| Empty tissue box | Small items, like: rocks, pinecones, balls, cotton balls, paper clips, erasers | Scissors (with an adult's help) | Construction paper |

LET'S TINKER!

Lay your materials next to each other. Can you think of other ways you can arrange your materials? **Use** these prepositions to rearrange your materials:

| across | behind | between | inside | next to | underneath |

LET'S MAKE: GUESSING BOX GAME!

1. Decorate an empty tissue box. You can **use** paper, glue, paint, and more.

2. Place a small item inside the box.

3. Find a partner. **Ask** him or her to guess what's inside. They can **ask** questions for clues: "Who does this belong to? What is it for? Where is it from? When would you use it?"

4. Still can't guess? **Tell** your partner to reach inside the box and keep asking questions, like "Why is it soft?"

5. Next it's your turn! **Close** your eyes while your partner puts a new material in the box. **Use** question words to get clues!

LET'S ENGINEER!

Enid keeps losing her toys inside her bedroom. She can't remember where to put things, and then she can't find her toys when she is ready to play.

How can Enid remember where to put her toys?

Draw, write, or make something that shows you where you keep your toys. If someone else looked at your solution, would they be able to find the toys? **Test** it out with a friend or family member.

PROJECT 6: DONE!
Get your sticker!

Working with Unknown Words

With the help of an adult, read the essay aloud. Circle the words in the essay that are new to you.

My Favorite Art Material

At school I learned to paint with watercolors! I like it because the paint can look see-through. It is watery and transparent.

To start, dip a brush in water. Use the wet bristles to move a drop of water onto the paints. (The paints start out dry and hard, but the water makes them soft and easier to use.) Last, put your brush on the paper and start painting.

I like to paint self-portraits. That means I make a picture of me! I also like to make abstract paintings. That means I paint colorful lines and shapes and dots that don't have to look like any special thing at all.

Watercolors are my favorite art material. I can't wait to paint again.

The writer describes watercolor paints as transparent, watery, and see-through.

Circle the paint below that is **transparent**.

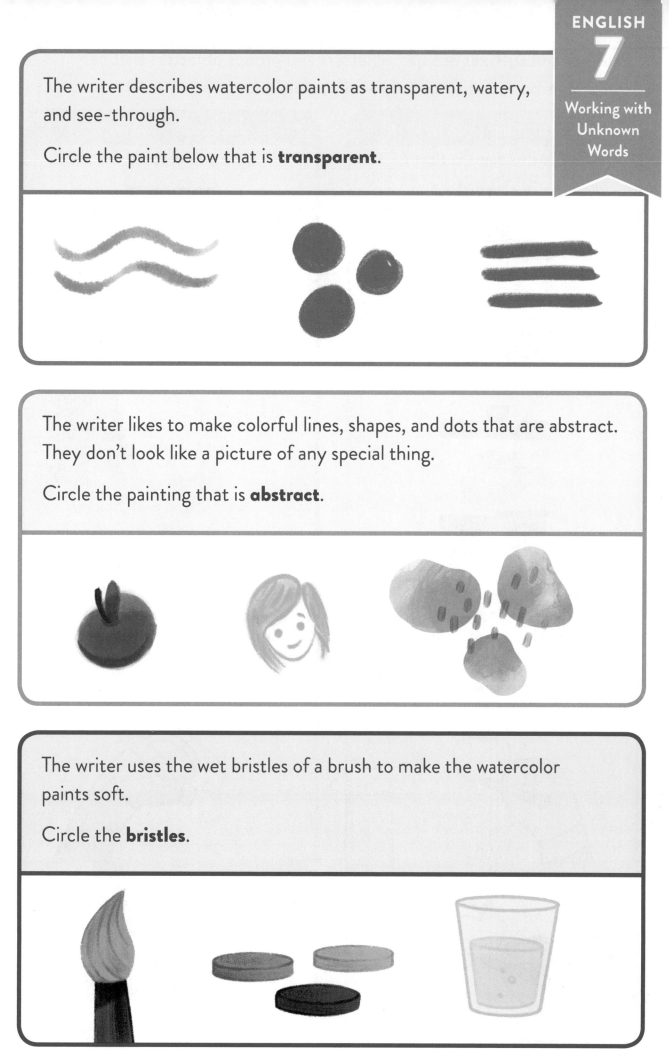

The writer likes to make colorful lines, shapes, and dots that are abstract. They don't look like a picture of any special thing.

Circle the painting that is **abstract**.

The writer uses the wet bristles of a brush to make the watercolor paints soft.

Circle the **bristles**.

Prefixes and **suffixes** are special letters and groups of letters that can sometimes be added to a word to make a new word.

-ful means full of

Circle the picture that is

colorful

-less means without

Circle the picture that is

nameless

re- means again

Circle the picture that shows

redraw

un- means not

Circle the picture that shows

undo

A **self-portrait** is a picture that you make of yourself. Draw a self-portrait with a pencil. Then, follow the instructions to add to your drawing.

Undo mistakes by using your eraser.

Redraw your head with a hat on.

Use crayons or markers to make your drawing **colorful**.

If your drawing is **nameless**, write your name at the bottom.

A **homograph** is a word that is spelled like another word but that is different in meaning. Read each sentence and look at the pictures. Then circle a different meaning of the homograph.

Callie is going to drop the paint.

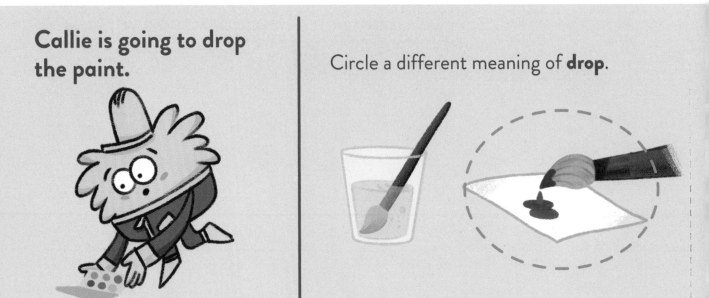

Circle a different meaning of **drop**.

Enid likes to ring the bell.

Circle a different meaning of **ring**.

Frank has to duck because of flying paint!

Circle a different meaning of **duck**.

Brian has a bat.

Circle a different meaning of **bat**.

The boat is going to sink.

Circle a different meaning of **sink**.

A wave is coming.

Move your body to show another meaning of **wave**. Then draw a picture of yourself waving.

LET'S START!

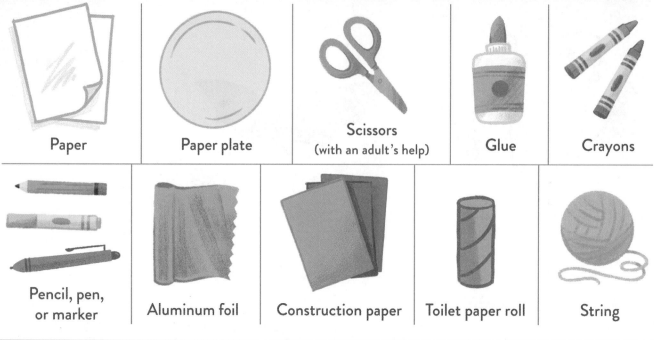

Paper	Paper plate	Scissors (with an adult's help)	Glue	Crayons
Pencil, pen, or marker	Aluminum foil	Construction paper	Toilet paper roll	String

LET'S TINKER!

Get a partner. First, **do** an action and say it aloud. **Jump**!

Your partner must **think** of a similar action to do and say the word. **Hop**!

Take turns going first. **Try** actions like run and sprint or walk and march. Who can think of the most? Did you hear any new words?

LET'S MAKE: COLOR WHEEL FLOWER!

1. **Draw** 3 straight lines across a paper plate.

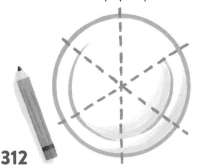

2. **Cut** the plate into 6 equal triangles.

3. **Make** 2 cuts at the top of each triangle to make a petal shape.

4. Look at the names of the colors on your crayons. **Find** 6 that are new to you and sound out their names.

5. Color each petal a different color. Then **write** the name on the petal with a pen or marker.

6. Lay your petals into a flower shape on a piece of paper, and then glue them down.

7. Draw a stem.

LET'S ENGINEER!

Dimitri is afraid of bats—the flying kind. So when Callie tells him that she bought a new bat, he runs the other way.

How can Callie show Dimitri the different meanings of bat?

Use your materials to show the two meanings of bat. How can you show the animal bat and the piece of sports equipment needed to play baseball? Can you also show the difference between an animal with a trunk and a car with a trunk?

PROJECT 7: DONE!
Get your sticker!

A **recipe** is a type of text that describes how to cook a food.
Read this recipe.

MotMot Power Smoothie

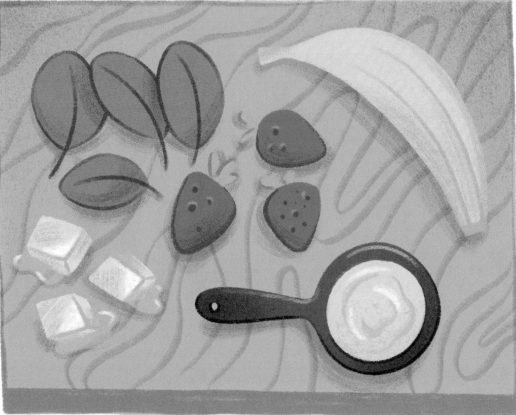

Ingredients:

6 strawberries

1 handful of
spinach leaves

1 banana

½ cup of yogurt

½ cup of ice

Steps:

1. First, wash the strawberries and spinach leaves in a sink.

2. Next, peel the banana.

3. Then, place all the ingredients into a blender with the help of an adult. Turn it on to blend until the ingredients are well mixed and smooth.

4. Last, pour the smoothie into cups. Enjoy!

Write the numbers 1, 2, 3, and 4 to put the recipe's illustrations in order from first to last.

Make your own smoothie recipe with your favorite fruits and vegetables. Write and draw your ideas below. Then read it aloud.

Recipe Title: _____

Author: _____

Ingredients: _____

_____

Steps: First, _____

_____

_____

_____

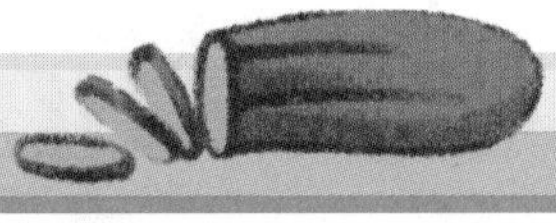

Next, _____

_____

_____

Then, _____

_____

_____

_____

Last, _____

_____

_____

_____

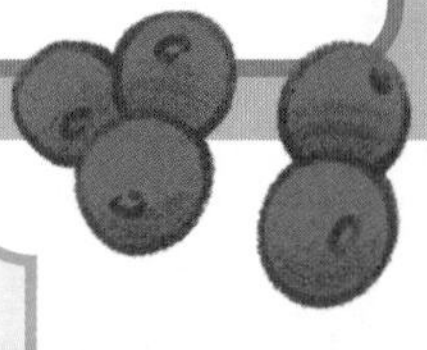

Share your recipe with an adult to make sure it would be safe, healthy, and yummy! Then try to make it together.

Frank and Dimitri have created a cookbook full of MotMot recipes. Circle the front cover. Draw a square around the back cover.

Find the front and back covers of this workbook!

Frank is the author of this cookbook. Dimitri is the illustrator. Write about and draw what job each MotMot did to create this cookbook.

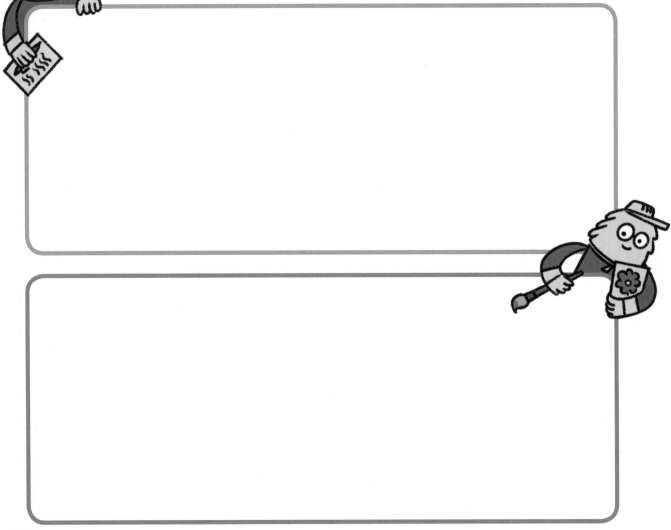

It's a busy day for reading in the Tinker Town park.

Color the newspaper **blue**. Color the storybook **red**.
Color the e-reader **yellow**. Color the map **green**.
Color the instruction manual **orange**.
Color the rest of the illustration as you like!

Hunt for other kinds of texts in your home, school, or library!

LET'S START! GATHER THESE TOOLS AND MATERIALS.

Some favorite books

Paper

Scissors
(with an adult's help)

Pencil

Crayons

LET'S TINKER!

Look at the books in your materials. **Find** the author and the illustrator in each book. **Point** at what the author did on each page. **Point** at what the illustrator did on each page. Can you find a book where one person did both jobs?

LET'S MAKE: FLAP BOOK!

1. Fold a piece of paper in half.

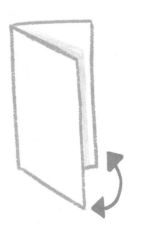

2. Make 3 cuts through half of the paper.

3. Draw 4 pictures that tell a story, 1 picture on each flap, from top to bottom.

4. Add your name as the author and illustrator.

5. On the paper underneath each flap, **write** what happens in each picture.

WINNER!

6. Share your book with a friend.

LET'S ENGINEER!

The MotMots wrote a story. They want to share it with their friends who live far away.

How can the MotMots use digital tools to share their writing with friends who are far away?

Gather a piece of your writing that you'd like to share—or make one! With the help of an adult, **send** it to a friend or family member who is somewhere else. **Think** about the different ways you can send something. What tools or materials do you need? **Ask** an adult for help. Can you share a picture to go with the writing?

PROJECT 8: DONE!
Get your sticker!

Reading Informational Texts

A **timeline** shows things that have happened in order from the past to the present. With the help of an adult, read the timeline aloud.

— Timeline of Bicycle History —

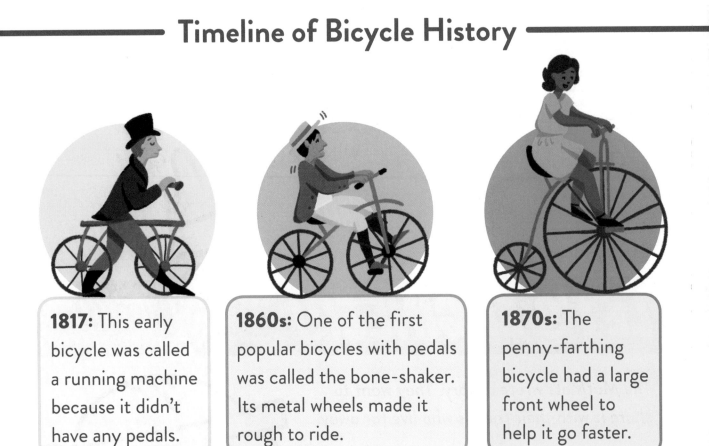

1817: This early bicycle was called a running machine because it didn't have any pedals.

1860s: One of the first popular bicycles with pedals was called the bone-shaker. Its metal wheels made it rough to ride.

1870s: The penny-farthing bicycle had a large front wheel to help it go faster.

Circle the bicycle that was invented first.

Put a ✔ next to the main idea of this timeline.

☐ Some bicycles don't have pedals.

☐ Bicycles have gone through many changes over time.

☐ Kids cannot ride bicycles.

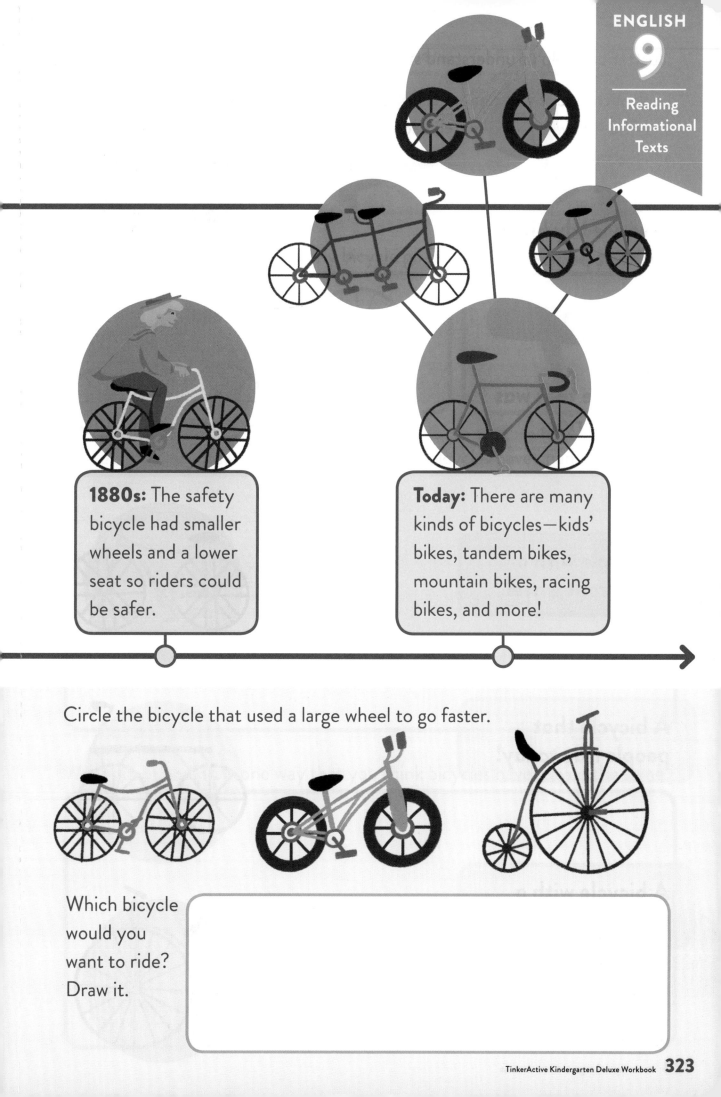

1880s: The safety bicycle had smaller wheels and a lower seat so riders could be safer.

Today: There are many kinds of bicycles—kids' bikes, tandem bikes, mountain bikes, racing bikes, and more!

Circle the bicycle that used a large wheel to go faster.

Which bicycle would you want to ride? Draw it.

Bicycles keep changing, even today. Some are being made from stronger and lighter materials. Some are being designed to go faster.

Draw a picture of what you think bicycles will look like in the future. Include yourself—and don't forget to add a helmet!

Where would you bike to? _____

Talk to a friend or an adult—tell them what you learned from the timeline about how bicycles have changed.

Write and draw your own timeline to show the order that things have happened from the past to the present.

My Day

When I woke up, I _____

_____.

In the morning, I _____

_____.

In the afternoon, I _____

_____.

At night, I _____

_____.

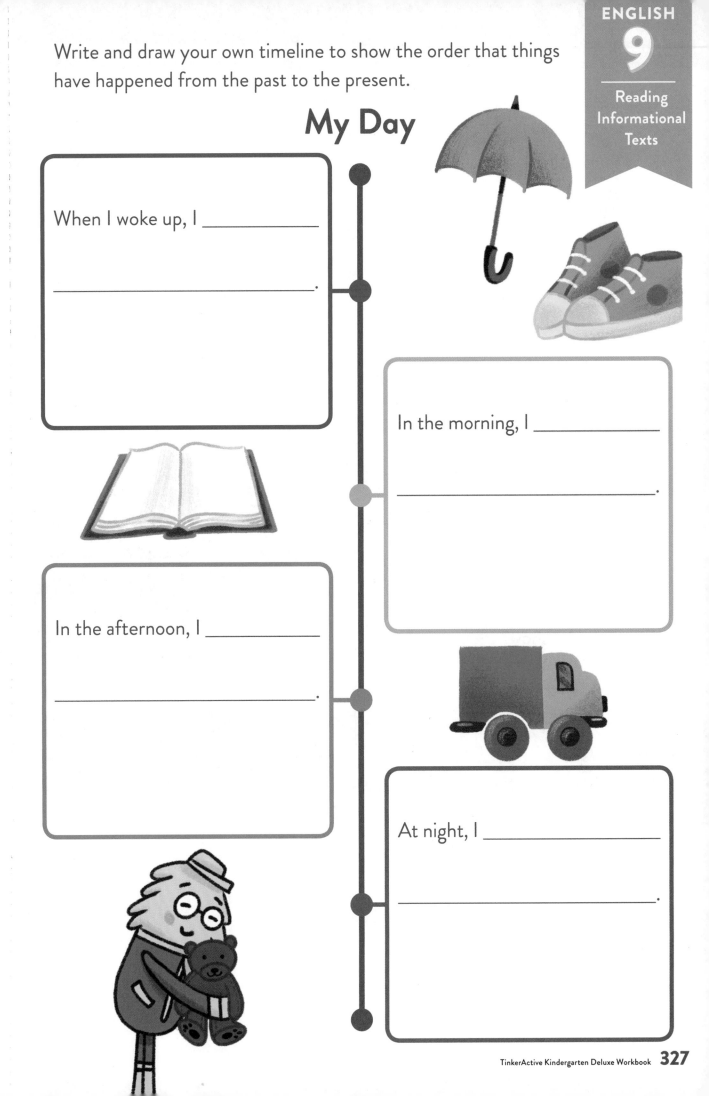

LET'S START!

GATHER THESE TOOLS AND MATERIALS.

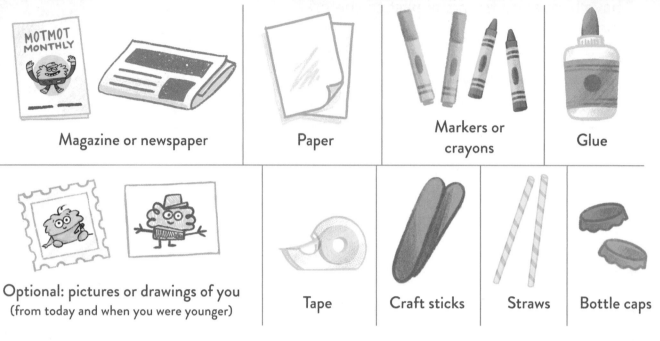

Magazine or newspaper	Paper	Markers or crayons
		Glue

Optional: pictures or drawings of you
(from today and when you were younger)

Tape

Craft sticks

Straws

Bottle caps

LET'S TINKER!

Flip through the pages of a magazine or newspaper. **Look** at the pictures to predict what the articles and stories may be about. Can you find any maps? Or a timeline? What do they show?

LET'S MAKE: TIMELINE OF YOUR LIFE!

1. Draw a line from the top to the bottom of a piece of paper.

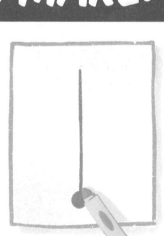

2. Draw or glue a baby picture at the top of the timeline. This marks when you were born.

3. **Draw** or glue a picture of you today at the bottom of the timeline. This marks the present, today.

4. **Add** more drawings and pictures to the timeline to show other important events in your life. **Place** them to show the order they happened. You can **include** when you started school, went on a trip, met a new friend, or any other important event.

LET'S ENGINEER!

Enid loves to bike around town, but her tricycle is not very fast. It has three wheels and sits very close to the ground.

How can Enid make her tricycle faster?

Build your own model of a fast bicycle, tricycle, or other vehicle Enid could ride. How can you use the materials to show wheels, pedals, handlebars, and a seat? What makes a vehicle fast? What other parts can you add or take away so your vehicle goes fast?

PROJECT 9: DONE!
Get your sticker!

Reading Literature

A **folktale** is a story that has been told by people over and over again. There are often many versions of the same story. With the help of an adult, read this folktale aloud.

Quackling the Duck

Quackling was a kind duck. When the king needed money, Quackling loaned him his coins. However, days and years passed, and the king never gave the coins back. So Quackling took an empty bag and headed to the castle.

Along the road, he ran into a ladder, a fox, and a beehive. The ladder yelled to him, "Quackling, are you headed to the castle?"

"Yes. The king has my coins, you see! Do you need a lift to the castle?" quacked the duck. The ladder, fox, and beehive all nodded, so Quackling put his friends in his bag for the trip.

When Quackling got to the castle, the king was upset—he did not want to give the coins back, because he was selfish. He told his guards to put Quackling in a deep hole. Quackling cried, "Quack! Quack! Quack! What will I do?" His friends heard him, and the ladder said, "Don't worry, Quackling. We'll help you!" And Quackling climbed up the ladder out of the hole.

The king was even more upset, so he told his guards to put Quackling into a pen with some angry chickens. Quackling said, "Quack! Quack! Quack! What will I do?" His friends heard him, and the fox said, "Don't worry, Quackling. We'll help you!" And the fox scared the chickens away.

The king grew even more upset, so he told his guards to bring Quackling into the castle. "I will sit on this duck. That's just his luck!" said the king. Quackling was very worried, and he moaned, "Quack!

Quack! Quack! What will I do?" His friends heard him, and the bees said, "Don't worry, Quackling. We'll help you!" The bees left the hive and flew toward the king. The king ran far, far away from the bees and was never seen again.

The guards and other people in the castle huddled around Quackling and his friends. "You are so kind!" they said. "And such a good friend!" They made Quackling their new king.

Circle the friends that went into Quackling's bag.

Circle what Quackling wanted to get from the king.

Circle the picture of how Quackling felt when the king threw him into a deep hole.

Write the numbers 1, 2, 3, and 4 to put the illustrations in order from first to last.

1 _____   _____   _____   _____

Stories like folktales have characters, settings, and events.

A **character** is a person or animal in a story.

A **setting** is a place in a story.

An **event** is an action that happens in a story.

Characters

Write two words that describe Quackling.

_____ _____

Write two words that describe the king.

_____ _____

Draw a picture of how Quackling treated the king.

Draw a picture of how the king treated Quackling.

Settings

Draw a picture of each setting.

> The road to the castle

> Inside the castle

Events

Draw a picture of each event.

The ladder helped Quackling escape from a deep hole.	The fox saved Quackling from angry chickens.	The king ran away from the bees.

Act out each of these events in the story with a friend or family member.

Write and draw to answer each question.

How was Quackling kind to the king?

How did Quackling treat his friends?

Why did the people make Quackling their king?

What lesson did Quackling learn about friendship? Talk about it with a friend or family member.

How do you and your friends show kindness to each other?

Draw a picture of you and your friends helping each other.

Find a friend or family member. Tell each other a
story about a time that you were a good friend.

LET'S START! GATHER THESE TOOLS AND MATERIALS.

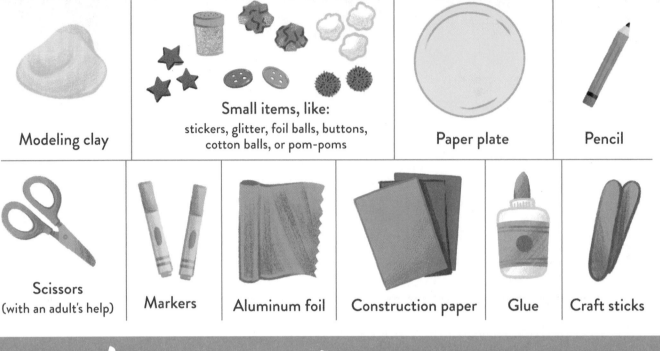

Modeling clay

Small items, like:
stickers, glitter, foil balls, buttons, cotton balls, or pom-poms

Paper plate

Pencil

Scissors
(with an adult's help)

Markers

Aluminum foil

Construction paper

Glue

Craft sticks

LET'S TINKER!

Make characters out of the clay. You can **make** Quackling and the king, or your own characters—people, animals, or objects. **Push** other materials into the clay to add features, like eyes. How many characters do you need to tell your own story? Do your characters talk? What do they say?

LET'S MAKE: QUACKLING'S CROWN!

1. **Draw** a 4-line star in the middle of a paper plate.

2. Fold the plate in half and cut along each of the lines. (Don't cut all the way to the plate's edge.) **Unfold** and cut along the last line as well.

3. Fold each of the triangles up to create a crown.

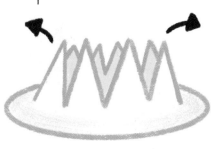

4. Decorate the crown using your materials.

LET'S ENGINEER!

The MotMots are putting on a show for their friends. They have lots of characters, but they don't have a setting. Their story could take place in a house, a school, a playground, a car, or even at the zoo!

How can they create a setting for the show?

Build a setting for your modeling clay characters using the materials. Where will your story take place? What items will you make to show where the setting is?

PROJECT 10: DONE!
Get your sticker!

A realistic fiction story is a story that could have happened in the real world but didn't. Read this realistic fiction story aloud.

The Friendly Ghosts

"Today is Halloween!" Nat said. "Time to buy a Halloween costume!" On his way out the door, he ran into his friend Joy. "Can I borrow your scissors?" she asked. Nat wanted to go to the store, but he wanted to help his friend, too. He decided to go back inside and get his scissors. "Thanks!" said Joy, and she walked off.

On his way out the door a second time, Nat ran into his friend Max. "Can I borrow a black marker?" he asked. Nat wanted to go to the store, but he wanted to help his friend, too. He decided to go back inside and get his black marker. "Thanks!" said Max.

On his way out the door a third time, Nat ran into his friend Liv. "Can I borrow some sheets?" she asked. Now Nat really needed to go to the store! It would be closing soon. But he wanted to help his friend. He decided to go back inside and get some sheets. "Thanks!" said Liv.

"Oh no!" thought Nat as he looked at his clock. "Trick-or-treating is starting, and I don't have time to get a costume!" He glumly sat down on his front steps. Suddenly a pack of ghosts walked up to him. One of them said, "Nat! This is for you!" Nat was confused. He took the white lump and unfolded it—it was a ghost costume! Then he looked closely at the ghosts—they were Joy, Max, and Liv! Nat put on his new costume and yelled, "Boo!" They all laughed and went trick-or-treating together.

Write and draw what you think Nat said to Joy when she asked to borrow his scissors.

Write and draw what you think Nat was thinking when his friends brought him the costume.

Compare the ghost costumes. What is the same? What is different? Circle two differences you see in each pair.

There are many types of stories. Read and compare the folktale "Quackling the Duck" (from page 330 and 331) with the realistic fiction story "The Friendly Ghosts" (from page 338).

The characters in both stories had good friends. Write the names of Quackling's friends and draw a picture of them with Quackling.

_____

_____

Write the names of Nat's friends and draw a picture of them with Nat.

_____

Compare "Quackling the Duck" with "The Friendly Ghosts."

QUACKLING

Write about and draw where Quackling was trying to go.

Write about and draw how Quackling helped his friends.

Write about and draw how Quackling's friends helped him.

How did Quackling feel when he put on the crown? Act it out!

NAT

Write about and draw where Nat was trying to go.

Write about and draw how Nat helped his friends.

Write about and draw how Nat's friends helped him.

How did Nat feel when he put on the ghost costume? Act it out!

LET'S START!

GATHER THESE TOOLS AND MATERIALS.

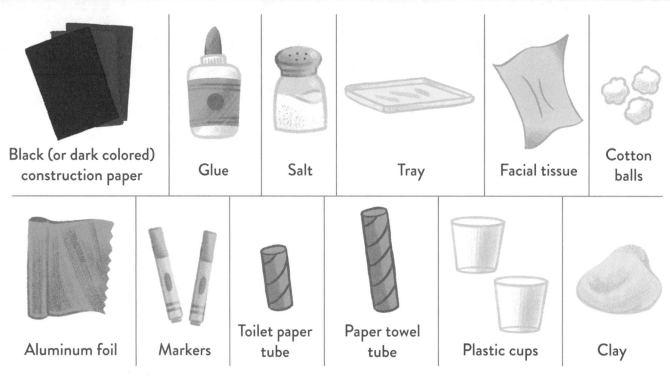

Black (or dark colored) construction paper

Glue

Salt

Tray

Facial tissue

Cotton balls

Aluminum foil

Markers

Toilet paper tube

Paper towel tube

Plastic cups

Clay

LET'S TINKER!

Pick two of your materials. **Look** at them closely and compare them. How are they the same? Do they have the same color, shape, texture, or weight? How are they different?

LET'S MAKE: SALTY GHOSTS!

1. Use glue to draw the outline of a ghost on a piece of dark paper.

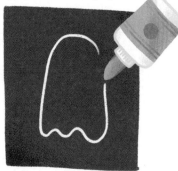

2. Draw eyes and a mouth with the glue.

3. Then **fill** in the ghost with glue—but don't fill in the eyes or the mouth!

4. Put your paper on a tray. **Dump** salt over the glue.

5. Start over again with a new piece of paper to make a second ghost. **Choose** a new shape and face so that the ghosts will be different from each other.

LET'S ENGINEER!

Dimitri and Enid are planning their Halloween costumes—they both want to dress like ghosts. They also want their costumes to be exactly the same, with no differences at all.

How can Dimitri and Enid make two ghost costumes that are exactly the same?

Use your materials to make models of two ghosts. Which materials will work the best? **Compare** the two ghosts—how are they the same? Do you see any differences? How can you change the ghosts or the way you make them so they are more alike?

PROJECT 11: DONE!
Get your sticker!

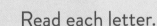
Read each letter.

To: Mia

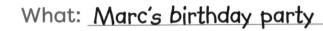

YOU ARE INVITED!

What: Marc's birthday party

When: Friday

Where: At my house

What to Wear: Dress up as an animal. I will wear my tiger costume.

Party Notes: There will be ice cream! What topping do you like?

From: Marc

Dear Marc,

Thank you for the invitation. And happy birthday! I also have a tiger costume! Is it okay if I wear it, too? I like blue sprinkles on my ice cream. I cannot wait for your party.

Sincerely,

Mia

• **Periods** are used at the end of a statement.
Draw a ◯ around the periods on page 346.

❓ **Question marks** are used when there is a question.
Draw a ▢ around the question marks on page 346.

❗ **Exclamation marks** are used when there is a big feeling, like excitement.
Draw a △ around the exclamation marks on page 346.

Circle the way a person would look when saying each sentence. Look at the punctuation for clues.

There will be ice cream!

What topping do you like?

Thanks for the ice cream.

Write about your own birthday.

Write a capital **I** to begin each sentence.

_____ have a birthday, too.

_____ celebrate my birthday every year.

_____ will turn one year older this year.

Write a capital **I** in each sentence. Then complete each sentence.

This year _____ will turn _____ years old.

On my birthday _____ feel _____.

One thing _____ like to do on my birthday is _____

_____.

Write a sentence about each MotMot on his or her birthday.
Use a capital letter for the first word of each sentence.
Use a . or ! to end each sentence.

_____

_____

_____

_____

_____

_____

Plan your own birthday party! Write words and punctuation to complete each sentence. Draw pictures to share your ideas.

MY PARTY!

Draw a picture of your decorations.

Write a list of people you will invite.

_____

_____

_____

_____

Write a sentence about the snacks you'd like at your party.

_____

_____

Write a sentence about the games you'd like at your party.

_____

_____

Write your own letter to tell your friends about your birthday party.

To: _____

YOU ARE INVITED!

What: _____

When: _____

Where: _____

What to Wear: _____

Party Notes: _____

_____

From: _____

Remember to use an **!** at the end of sentences that you are excited about.

Draw a picture of yourself on your birthday.

Construction paper	Markers	Scissors (with an adult's help)	Hole punch
String	Magazine and newspapers		Glue

LET'S TINKER!

Get three pieces of construction paper and write one punctuation mark on each: **. ! ?**

Grab a partner and play a guessing game. First **have** your partner make a face. Then **hold** up the punctuation mark that matches.

A straight face gets a "**.**" A strong emotion gets an "**!**" And a confused expression gets a "**?**"

Who can guess the most faces correctly?

LET'S MAKE: BIG LETTER BANNER!

1. Cut large triangles out of construction paper. **Make** the same number of triangles as letters in your name.

2. Punch 2 holes in 1 side of each triangle.

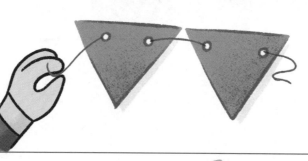

3. Thread them onto the string to make a banner.

4. Flip through magazines and newspapers. **Find** capital letters at the start of sentences and cut them out. Can you find all the letters in your name?

5. Glue the capital letters onto the banner to spell your name.

LET'S ENGINEER!

So many friends and family members came to Callie's birthday party. She wants to thank them all again and tell them how special her birthday was—but they've all gone home.

How can Callie thank her friends and family?

Make your own thank-you note using the materials. **Write** the name of a person you'd like to write the note to. Then **write** a sentence to describe what you are thankful for. **Decorate** your note. With the help of an adult, **send** it!

PROJECT 12: DONE!
Get your sticker!

Telling a Story

A **myth** is a traditional story that explains something people see around them that they don't understand. With the help of an adult, read the myth aloud.

The Myth of Nian

Nian was a monster that lived in the mountains. Every Chinese New Year, he would become very hungry. Nian went to nearby villages to eat— sometimes he even ate the people! The villagers ran away because they were so afraid of Nian.

One year the villagers decided to work together to scare the monster away. They wore bright red robes and carried red lanterns. They lit up crackling fireworks, played loud drums, and banged on plates and bowls to make noise. When the monster appeared, he saw the bright red colors and fire and heard the loud noises. He was so afraid that he never returned to the village again! To this day, part of the Chinese New Year tradition includes red decorations, fireworks, and dances with loud drums.

Draw a picture of where Nian may have lived.

Draw a picture of how the villagers looked when they saw the monster.

Draw a picture of what a villager may have worn to scare away Nian.

"The Myth of Nian" tells what happened to the monster Nian.

First, Nian was hungry, so he ate food and people in the nearby village.

Next, the people wore red, lit fireworks, and made lots of noise.

Last, Nian was scared away and never came back!

Write and draw a story of your own by telling what happened first, next, and last. Start by giving your story a title.

Title: _____

First, _____

_____

Next, _____

_____

Last, _____

_____

LET'S START!

GATHER THESE TOOLS AND MATERIALS.

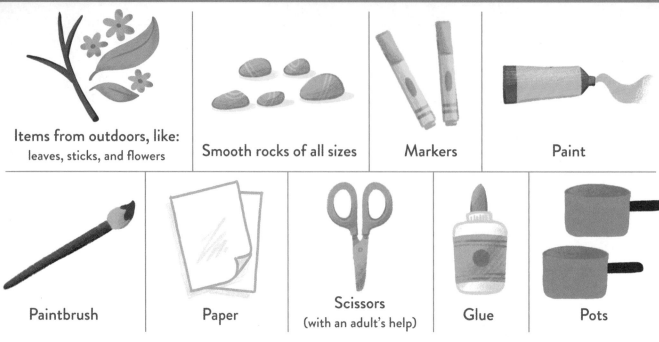

Items from outdoors, like: leaves, sticks, and flowers	Smooth rocks of all sizes	Markers	Paint
Paintbrush	Paper	Scissors (with an adult's help)	Glue	Pots

LET'S TINKER!

Think about your favorite memory from today. Where did it happen? What did you say and do? **Use** your materials to help act it out and tell the story to a friend.

LET'S MAKE: STORY ROCKS!

1. Wash and dry a smooth rock.

2. Use a marker to draw a face. **Add** other body parts to make your character—like horns, fins, or wings.

3. Use paint and a paintbrush to add colors to the rock, and then let the paint dry. You can also **use** stickers from page 389.

4. Paint more rocks to make more characters.

5. Tell your own story using your characters!

LET'S ENGINEER!

In "The Myth of Nian," the villagers used bright colors and loud noises to scare the monster Nian back to his mountain. The MotMots think there may be a monster hiding in their own Mount Ten!

How can they build their own tools to scare away monsters?

Build your own tools to scare away monsters. Which materials can be used to make noise? Which materials can make bright colors? What else can you build to scare away a monster?

MONSTERS, GO AWAY!

PROJECT 13: DONE!
Get your sticker!

Writing Informational Texts

Diagrams can be used to share information so that it is easy to understand. With the help of an adult, read the **Venn diagram**—it uses circles to group sets together.

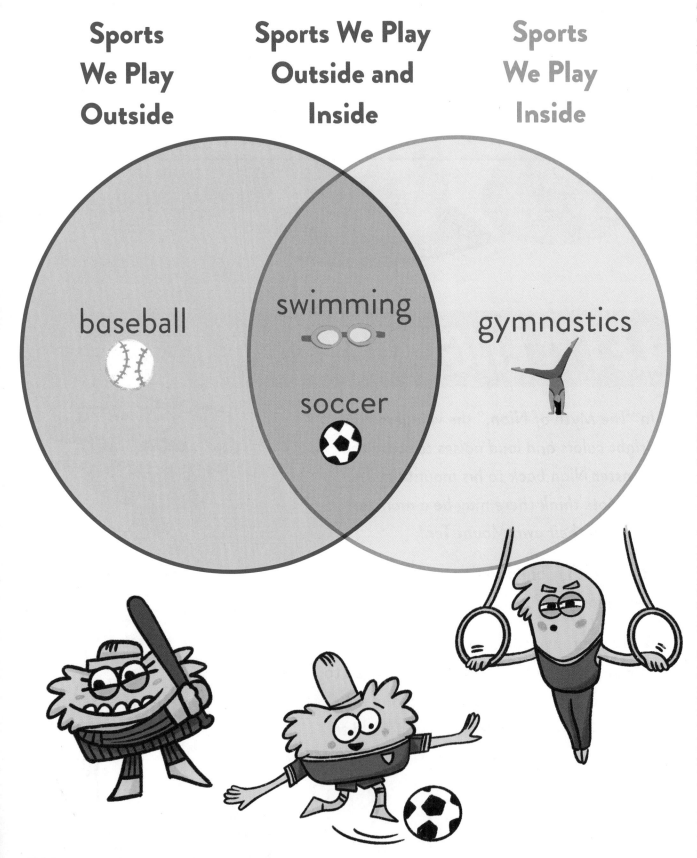

Sports We Play Outside

Sports We Play Outside and Inside

Sports We Play Inside

baseball

swimming

soccer

gymnastics

Use the information from the diagram to answer each question.

Circle the gear Frank can use to play inside.

Circle where the MotMots play baseball.

Inside

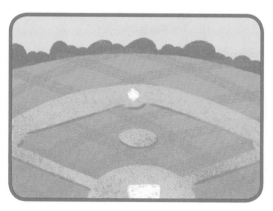

Outside

Make your own diagram of the sports and games that you like to play. Write and draw in each section of the Venn diagram.

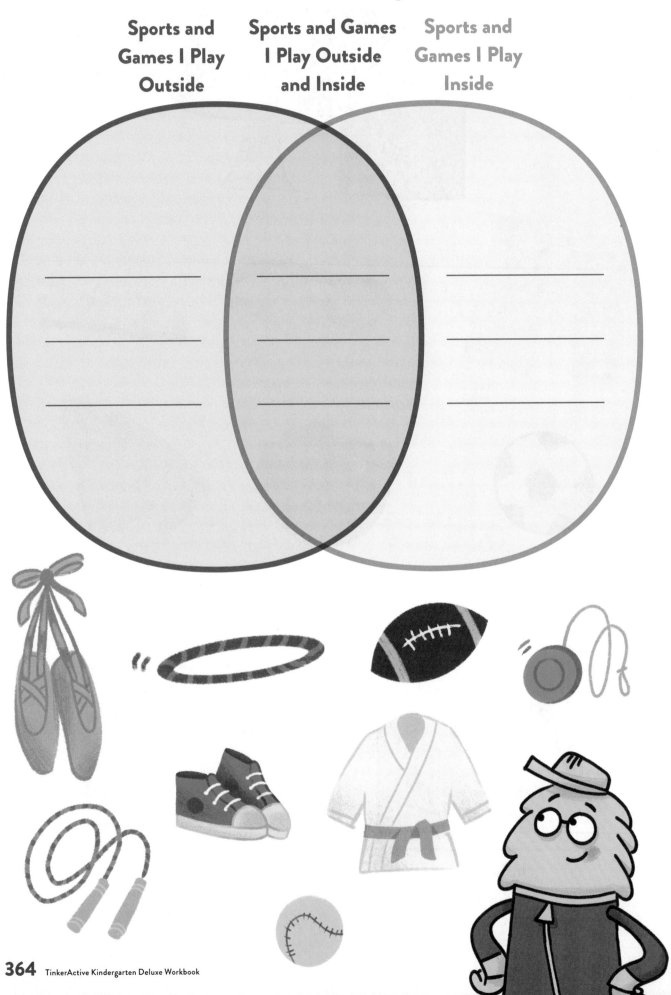

Sports and Games I Play Outside

Sports and Games I Play Outside and Inside

Sports and Games I Play Inside

Write and draw to share information about what you like to play.

One sport or game I like to play is _____.

A picture of me playing the sport or game:

The person who taught me to play this sport or game was _____

_____.

One thing you must know in order to play is _____

_____.

The gear I use to play is _____.

A picture of the gear I use:

Write and draw to share information about your favorite things.

My Favorites

My favorite food is _____.

A picture of my favorite food:

My favorite toy is _____.

A picture of my favorite toy:

My favorite place to go is _____.

A picture of me in my favorite place:

The best way to get there:

(Circle your answer.)

My favorite book is _____.

This is my favorite book because _____

_____.

Find an adult and share your favorites by reading them aloud. Ask other people in your family about their favorites, too!

LET'S START!

GATHER THESE TOOLS AND MATERIALS.

Paper	Paper plates	Magazines or newspapers
Dried foods, like: pasta, rice, and raisins	Glue	Scissors (with an adult's help)

LET'S TINKER!

Ask each person in your family about their favorite things—like animals, games, or books. **Write** or draw your discoveries on a piece of paper. Do any people share the same favorites as you?

LET'S MAKE: YUMMY PLATE!

1. Draw pictures of your favorite foods, cut pictures of them out of magazines, or get some actual dried foods, like pasta, rice, or raisins, from your kitchen.

2. Glue them to a paper plate.

3. Show your favorite foods to a friend or family member, and tell that person why they are your favorites.

LET'S ENGINEER!

Amelia is starting at a new school and meeting lots of new friends. She wants to show people some of her favorite things.

How can Amelia show her new friends what she likes and doesn't like?

Make a diagram that shows what you like and don't like. You can **write** and draw or glue pictures you have cut out of magazines and newspapers. What kind of diagram would work best? **Share** it with a new friend!

FOOD

ANIMALS

PROJECT 14: DONE!
Get your sticker!

A **biography** is the story of a real person's life, written by someone else. With the help of an adult, read the biography aloud.

Amelia Earhart

Amelia Earhart was born over one hundred years ago, in 1897. When she was a kid, Amelia liked to climb trees, play football, and go fishing. When she was twenty-three years old, she watched an air show and wanted to learn more about airplanes. Later, she took her first ride in an airplane, and it changed her life. Amelia started flying lessons and got her pilot's license.

As she gained more experience, Amelia started breaking records. She flew higher than other women had ever flown. She was even the first woman pilot to fly all the way across the Atlantic Ocean! She became famous all over the world for being brave and determined.

When she was thirty-nine years old, Amelia flew off on a long journey. She had one goal— to become the first woman to fly all the way around the world. She had almost completed her goal when one day she and her plane disappeared. After weeks of searching, no one could find Amelia or her plane. To this day no one knows for sure what happened. But Amelia Earhart will always be remembered for inspiring people to achieve their goals.

Circle a word that describes Amelia:

brave   bored   greedy

Draw a ✔ next to something Amelia did when she was a kid.

☐ She went for her first ride in an airplane.

☐ She went fishing outside.

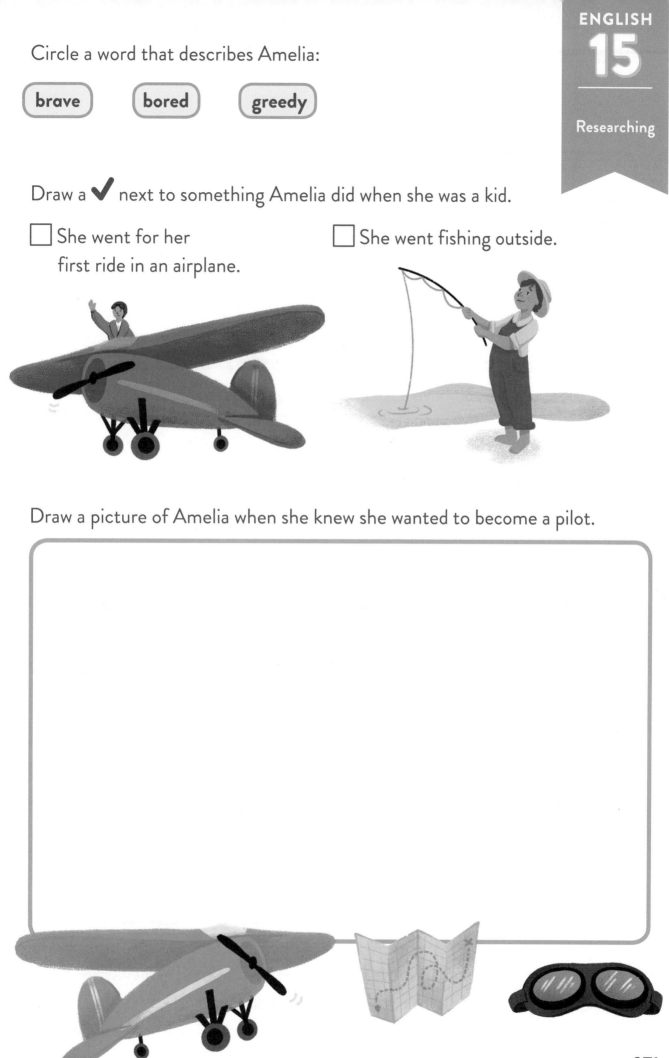

Draw a picture of Amelia when she knew she wanted to become a pilot.

Write and draw the questions you have after reading Amelia Earhart's biography.

What do you wonder about Amelia Earhart when she was a kid?

_____

What questions do you have about Amelia's airplane?

_____

What is something you want to know about how Amelia and her plane disappeared?

_____

Ask an adult to help you do research to learn more about Amelia Earhart. You could look for books at the library or research on the computer.

A **biography** is the story of a real person's life, written by someone else. An **autobiography** is the story of a real person's life, written by that person. You can write an autobiography about your life.

Ask your family and friends research questions about your life. Then write and draw what you learn below.

My birthday is _____.

My first food was _____.

I thought it tasted _____.

The first word I said was _____.

A drawing of me as a baby with my favorite toys:

Write about and draw important parts of your life.

I live at this address: _____.

The school I go to is _____.

My teacher's name is _____.

A picture or drawing of me at school:

The people in my family are _____

_____.

A picture or drawing of my family:

Write and draw your own autobiography—the story of your life. Use the research you've gathered on the previous pages. You can also write about and draw other memories and events.

My Autobiography

_____

_____

_____

_____

_____

_____

_____

LET'S START! GATHER THESE TOOLS AND MATERIALS.

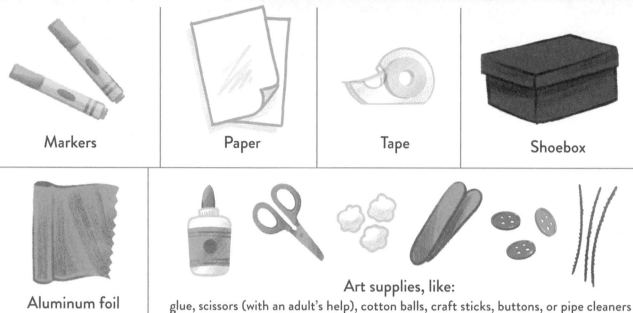

Markers

Paper

Tape

Shoebox

Aluminum foil

Art supplies, like:
glue, scissors (with an adult's help), cotton balls, craft sticks, buttons, or pipe cleaners

LET'S TINKER!

Go outside and find an interesting plant. **Use** your senses to become an expert: What does it look like, smell like, sound like, and feel like? Is it safe to taste? **Ask** an adult to be sure. How else can you learn more about it? **Write** and draw to record what you've learned.

LET'S MAKE: PAPER FLYER!

1. Fold a piece of paper in half. Then **open** it again.

2. Fold the top 2 corners down to meet in the middle.

3. Fold the upper left and right corner to meet in the middle.

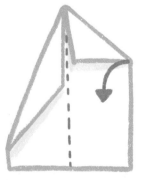

4. Fold the paper in half.

5. Fold each half down toward the outside to create wings.

6. Open up the wings, and put a piece of tape on the top to keep them together.

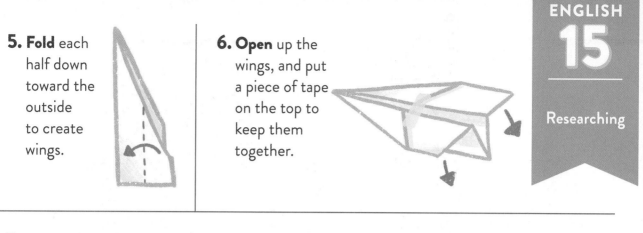

7. Use stickers from page 389 to decorate your plane. Now your airplane is ready to fly like Amelia Earhart's!

Observe how it flies. Can you make any changes to the airplane to make it fly farther?

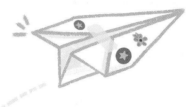

LET'S ENGINEER!

The MotMots have been reading biographies, including the one about Amelia Earhart. They are learning lots of details about people's lives.

How can the MotMots share with other people about their own lives without writing autobiographies?

Make a diorama about your life! **Build** models and draw the things that you see, hear, smell, and feel around you. **Use** your materials and/or gather items from outside to make pictures of the things around you in your life. Will you show models of any people? What places will you show? What other kinds of research about your life will you include?

PROJECT 15: DONE!
Get your sticker!

ANSWER KEY

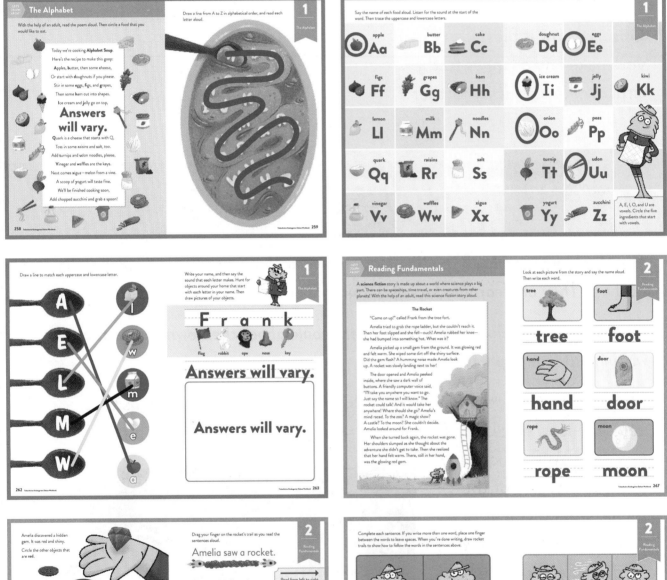

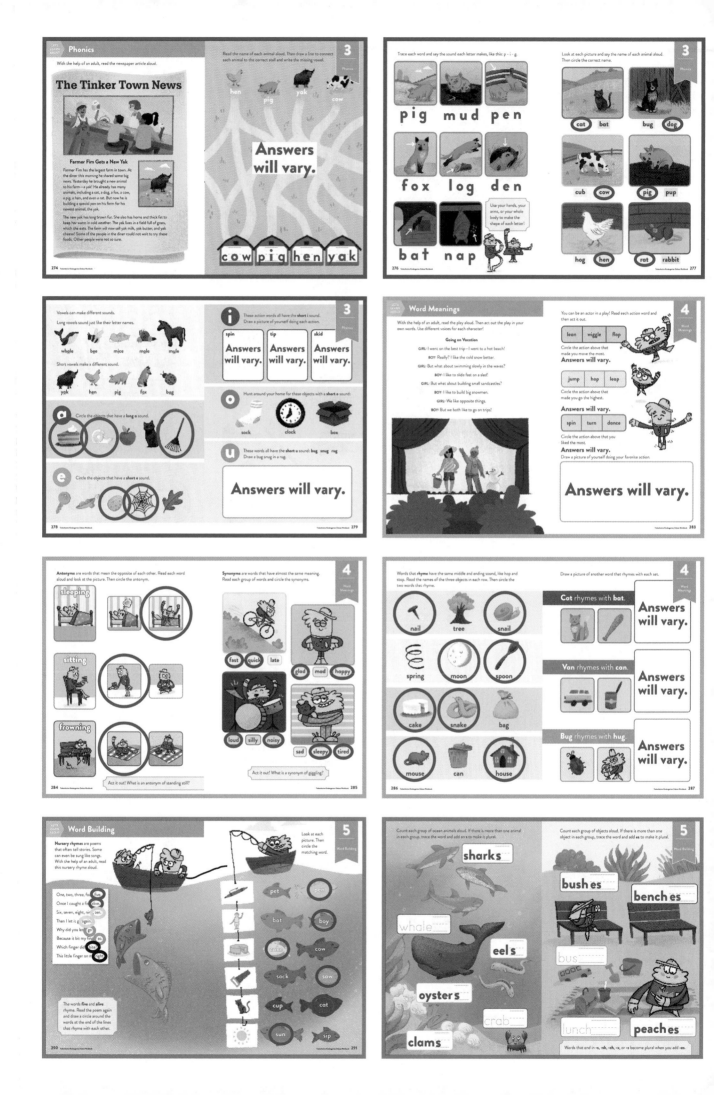

Phonics — 3

With the help of an adult, read the newspaper article aloud.

The Tinker Town News

Farmer Fim Gets a New Yak

Farmer Fim has the largest farm in town. At the diner this morning he shared some big news. Yesterday he brought a new animal to his farm—a yak! He already has many animals, including a cat, a dog, a fox, a cow, a pig, a ham, and even a rat. But now he is building a special pen on his farm for his newest animal, the yak.

The new yak has long brown fur. She also has horns and thick fat to keep her warm in cold weather. The yak lives in a field full of grass, which she eats. The farm will now sell yak milk, yak butter, and yak cheese! Some of the people in the diner could not wait to try these foods. Other people were not so sure.

Read the name of each animal aloud. Then draw a line to connect each animal to the correct stall and write the missing vowel.

hen   pig   yak   cow

Answers will vary.

c o w   p i g   h e n   y a k

Trace each word and say the sound each letter makes, like this: p - i - g.

pig   mud   pen
fox   log   den
bat   nap

Use your hands, your arms, or your whole body to make the shape of each letter!

Look at each picture and say the name of each animal aloud. Then circle the correct name.

cat   **bat**   bug   **dog**
cub   **cow**   **pig**   pup
hog   **hen**   rat   **rabbit**

Phonics — 3

Vowels can make different sounds.

Long vowels sound just like their letter names.

whale   bee   mice   mole   mule

Short vowels make a different sound.

yak   hen   pig   fox   bug

a Circle the objects that have a **long a** sound.

e Circle the objects that have a **short e** sound.

These action words all have the **short i** sound. Draw a picture of yourself doing each action.

spin   tip   skid

Answers will vary. **Answers will vary.** **Answers will vary.**

o Hunt around your home for these objects with a **short o** sound.

sock   clock   box

u These words all have the **short u** sound: bug snug rug
Draw a bug snug in a rug.

Answers will vary.

Word Meanings — 4

With the help of an adult, read the play aloud. Then act out the play in your own words. Use different voices for each character!

Going on Vacation

GIRL: I went on the best trip—I went to a hot beach!
BOY: Really? I like the cold snow better.
GIRL: But what about swimming slowly in the waves?
BOY: I like to slide fast on a sled!
GIRL: But what about building small sandcastles?
BOY: I like to build big snowmen.
GIRL: We like opposite things.
BOY: But we both like to go on trips!

You can be an actor in a play! Read each action word and then act it out.

lean   wiggle   flop

Circle the action above that made you move the most.
Answers will vary.

jump   hop   leap

Circle the action above that made you go the highest.
Answers will vary.

spin   turn   dance

Circle the action above that you liked the most.
Answers will vary.

Draw a picture of yourself doing your favorite action.

Answers will vary.

Word Meanings — 4

Antonyms are words that mean the opposite of each other. Read each word aloud and look at the picture. Then circle the antonym.

sleeping
sitting
frowning

Act it out! What is an antonym of standing still?

Synonyms are words that have almost the same meaning. Read each group of words and circle the synonyms.

fast   quick   late
glad   mad   happy
loud   silly   noisy
sad   sleepy   tired

Act it out! What is a synonym of giggling?

Word Meanings — 4

Words that **rhyme** have the same middle and ending sound, like hop and stop. Read the names of the three objects in each row. Then circle the two words that rhyme.

nail   tree   snail
spring   moon   spoon
cake   snake   bag
mouse   can   house

Draw a picture of another word that rhymes with each set.

Cat rhymes with bat.   **Answers will vary.**

Van rhymes with can.   **Answers will vary.**

Bug rhymes with hug.   **Answers will vary.**

Word Building — 5

Nursery rhymes are poems that often tell stories. Some can even be sung like songs. With the help of an adult, read this nursery rhyme aloud.

One, two, three, four, five,
Once I caught a fish alive,
Six, seven, eight, nine, ten,
Then I let it go again.
Why did you let it go?
Because it bit my finger so.
Which finger did it bite?
This little finger on my right.

The words **five** and **alive** rhyme. Read the poem again and draw a circle around the words at the end of the lines that rhyme with each other.

Look at each picture. Then circle the matching word.

pet   **pen**
bat   boy
cake   cow
sock   saw
cup   **cat**
sun   sip

Word Building — 5

Count each group of ocean animals aloud. If there is more than one animal in each group, trace the word and add an **s** to make it plural.

sharks
whale
eels
oysters
crab
clams

Count each group of objects aloud. If there is more than one object in each group, trace the word and add **es** to make it plural.

bushes
benches
bus
lunch
peaches

Words that end in -s, -sh, -ch, -x, or -z become plural when you add -es.

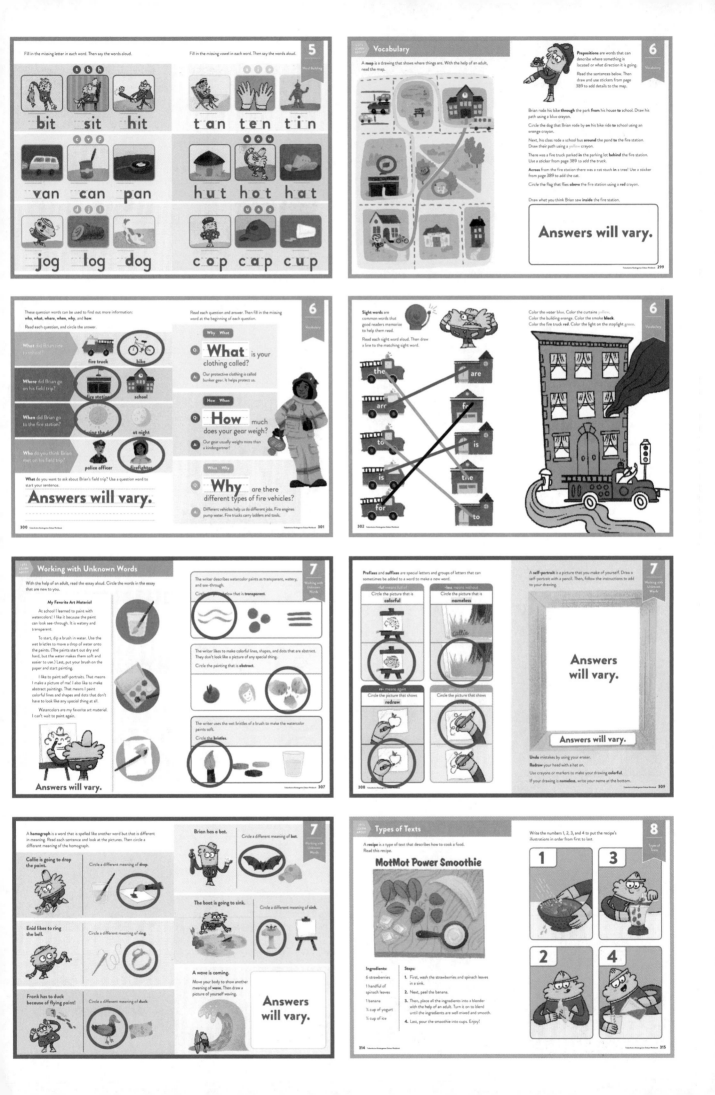

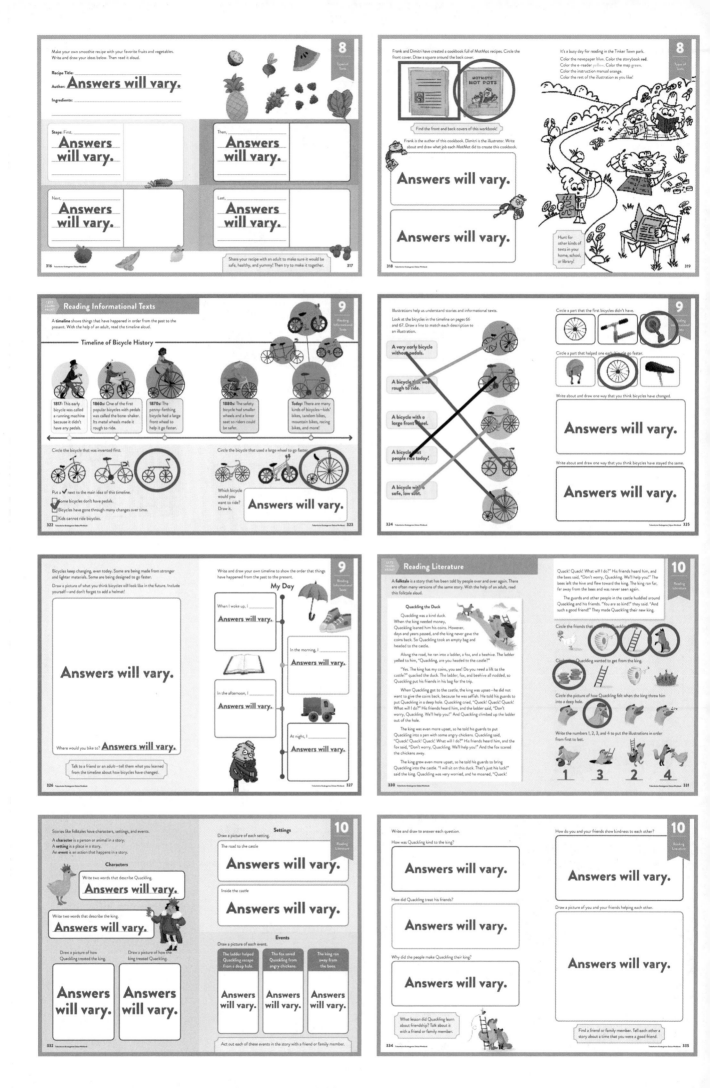

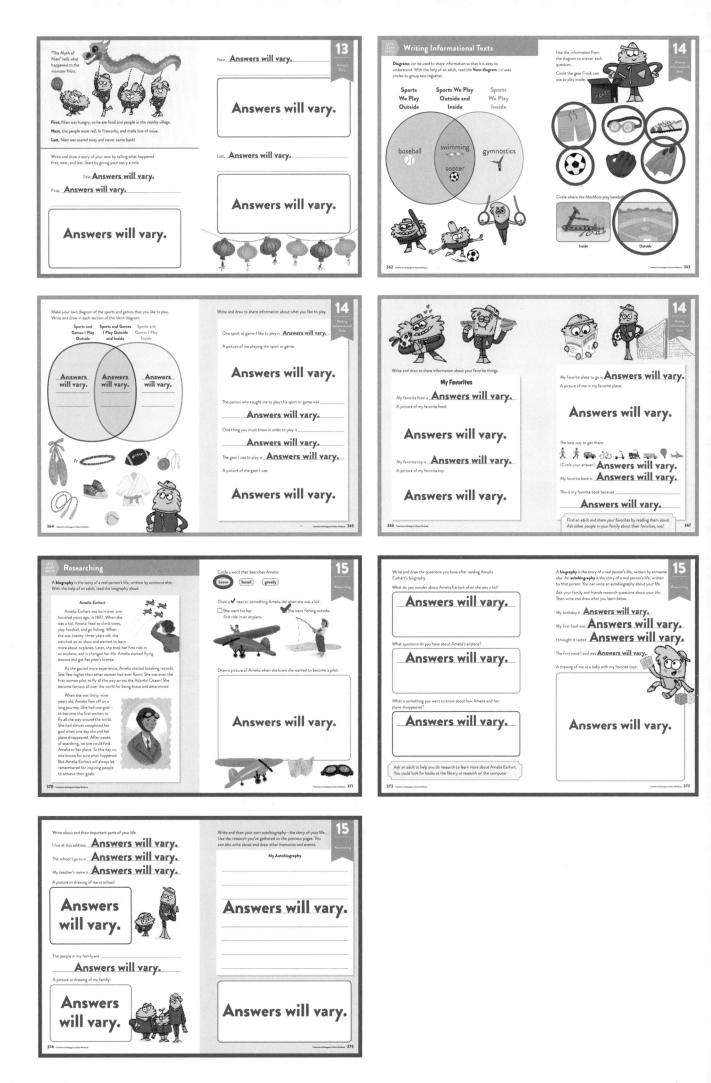

Odd Dot
120 Broadway
New York, NY 10271
OddDot.com

ISBN: 978-1-250-88474-9

WRITERS   Nathalie Le Du and Megan Hewes Butler

ILLUSTRATORS   Ellen Stubbings, Taryn Johnson, and Bronwyn Gruet

EDUCATIONAL CONSULTANT   Randi House

CHARACTER DESIGNER   Anna-Maria Jung

LEAD SERIES DESIGNER   Carolyn Bahar

INTERIOR DESIGNERS   Carolyn Bahar and Tim Hall

COVER DESIGNER   Caitlyn Hunter

EDITORS   Justin Krasner and Nathalie Le Du

Our books may be purchased in bulk for promotional, educational, or business use. Please contact your local bookseller or the Macmillan Corporate and Premium Sales Department at (800) 221-7945 ext. 5442 or by email at MacmillanSpecialMarkets@macmillan.com.

DISCLAIMER
The publisher and authors disclaim responsibility for any loss, injury, or damages
that may result from a reader engaging in the activities described in this book.

TinkerActive is a trademark of Odd Dot.
Printed in China by Dream Colour (Hong Kong) Printing Limited, Guangdong Province
First published for special markets in 2020
First trade edition, 2023

10 9 8 7 6 5 4 3 2 1

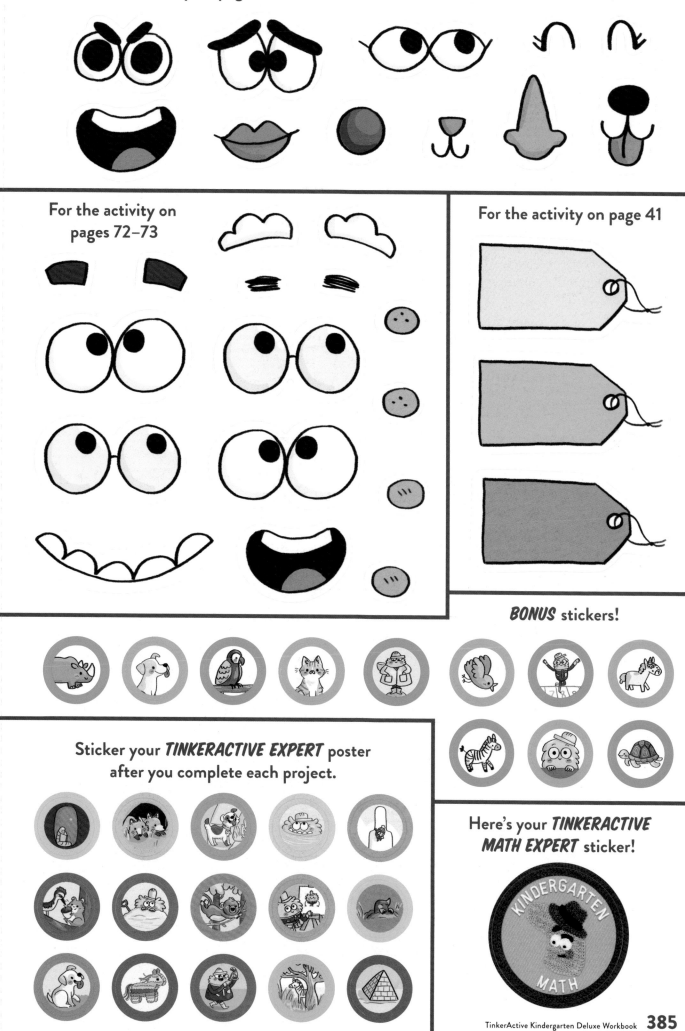

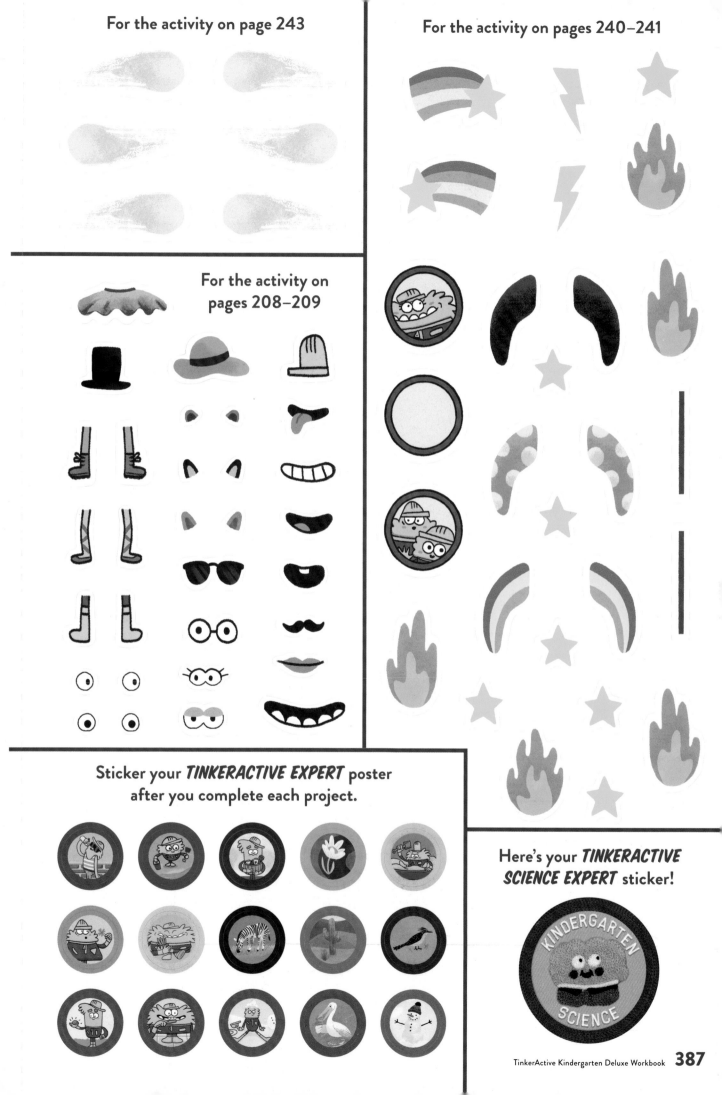

For the activity on page 243

For the activity on pages 240–241

For the activity on
pages 208–209

Sticker your *TINKERACTIVE EXPERT* poster
after you complete each project.

Here's your *TINKERACTIVE
SCIENCE EXPERT* sticker!

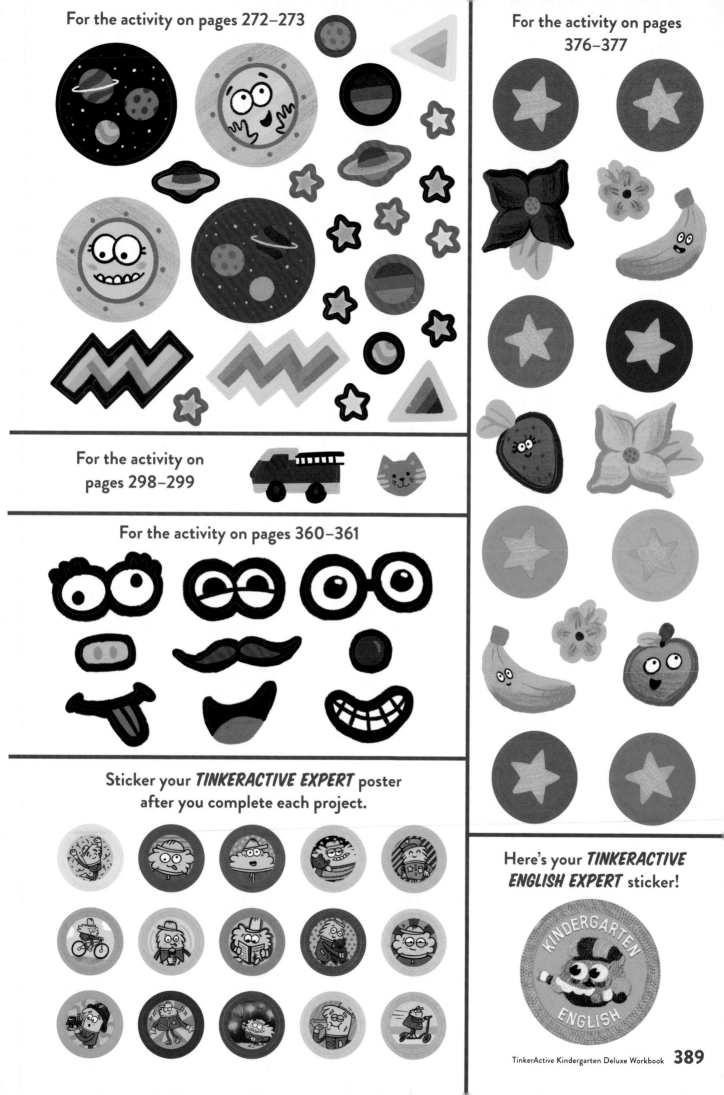

For the activity on pages 272–273

For the activity on pages 298–299

For the activity on pages 360–361

Sticker your **TINKERACTIVE EXPERT** poster after you complete each project.

For the activity on pages 376–377

Here's your **TINKERACTIVE ENGLISH EXPERT** sticker!

KINDERGARTEN ENGLISH